NUTRITION AND FITNESS

MACMILLAN

HEALTH

ENCYCLOPEDIA

4

Nutrition and Fitness

MACMILLAN PUBLISHING COMPANY
NEW YORK

MAXWELL MACMILLAN CANADA
TORONTO

MAXWELL MACMILLAN INTERNATIONAL
NEW YORK   OXFORD   SINGAPORE   SYDNEY

MACMILLAN
HEALTH
ENCYCLOPEDIA

4

EDITORIAL CREDITS

Developed and produced by
Visual Education Corporation, Princeton, NJ

Project Editor: Darryl Kestler

Editors: Richard Bohlander, Susan Garver,
Michael Gee, Emilie McCardell,
Cynthia Mooney, Suzanne Murdico,
Frances Wiser

Editorial Assistant: Carol Ciaston

Photo Editors: Maryellen Costa, Michael Gee

Photo Research: Cynthia Cappa, Sara Matthews

Production Supervisor: Anita Crandall

Proofreading Management: Amy Davis

Art Editors: Maureen Pancza, Mary Lyn Sodano

Advisor, Anatomical Illustrations:
David Seiden, Ph.D.
Robert Wood Johnson Medical School
Piscataway, New Jersey

Layout: Maxson Crandall, Lisa Evans

Word Processing: Cynthia Feldner

Design: Hespenheide Design

The information contained in the *Macmillan Health Encyclopedia* is not intended to take the place of the care and advice of a physician or health-care professional. Readers should obtain professional advice in making health-care decisions.

Macmillan Publishing Company
866 Third Avenue
New York, NY 10022

Maxwell Macmillan Canada, Inc.
1200 Eglinton Avenue East, Suite 200
Don Mills, Ontario M3C 3N1

Macmillan Publishing Company is part of the Maxwell Communication Group of Companies

Printed in the United States of America

printing number
1 2 3 4 5 6 7 8 9 10

PHOTO CREDITS

Jacket: Howard Sochurek/The Stock Market

Tom Dunham: 9 (top), 11, 18 (top), 19, 22 (both), 27, 29, 31, 36, 42, 43, 47, 51 (all), 54, 58, 63, 66, 67, 70, 76, 78, 82, 87, 89, 92, 96 (bottom), 98, 101, 106, 108 (right), 111, 114, 115, 118, 119, 120 (both), 124, 133

F-Stock Photo Agency: John Laptad, 96 (top); Caroline Wood, 107

George White Location Photography: 33

inStock: Philip Slagter, 74

Leo de Wys, Inc.: Steve Brown, 12; Alan Dolgins, 84; Paul Kennedy, 25 (top); David Lissy, 68

Richard B. Levine: 4

David Madison: 5; David Madison/DUOMO, 7; Shelby Thorner, 85

mga/PHOTRI: Frank Siteman, 52

PhotoEdit: 35, 88; Robert Brenner, 26, 41 (top); Jose Carrillo, 25 (bottom); Myrleen Ferguson, 18 (bottom); Tony Freeman, 9 (bottom left), 44, 62, 69, 93, 112, 123; Michael Newman, 131; Alan Oddie, 16 (right); David Young-Wolff, 41 (bottom), 50, 86, 127

The Picture Cube: Kindra Clineff, 95

Southern Stock Photo Agency: Winsett, 71

Unicorn Stock Photos: Steve Bourgeois, 49; Jay Foreman, 16 (left); Martha McBride, 40, 108 (left); Tom McCarthy, 105; C. Schmeiser, 9 (bottom right)

Library of Congress Cataloging-in-Publication Data
Macmillan health encyclopedia.
    v. <1–   >
    Includes index.
    Contents: v. 1. Body systems—v. 2. Communicable diseases—v. 3. Noncommunicable diseases and disorders—v. 4 Nutrition and fitness—v. 5. Emotional and mental health—v. 6. Sexuality and reproduction—v. 7. Drugs, alcohol, and tobacco—v. 8. Safety and environmental health—v. 9. Health-care systems/cumulative index
    ISBN 0-02-897439-5 (set).—ISBN 0-02-897431-X (v. 1).—ISBN 0-02-897432-8 (v. 2).
    1. Health—Encyclopedias.   I. Macmillan Publishing Company.
RA776.M174   1993
610′ .3—dc20   92-28939
                                    CIP

Volumes of the *Macmillan Health Encyclopedia*

1 *Body Systems* (ISBN 0-02-897431-X)
2 *Communicable Diseases* (ISBN 0-02-897432-8)
3 *Noncommunicable Diseases and Disorders* (ISBN 0-02-897433-6)
4 *Nutrition and Fitness* (ISBN 0-02-897434-4)
5 *Emotional and Mental Health* (ISBN 0-02-897435-2)
6 *Sexuality and Reproduction* (ISBN 0-02-897436-0)
7 *Drugs, Alcohol, and Tobacco* (ISBN 0-02-897437-9)
8 *Safety and Environmental Health* (ISBN 0-02-897438-7)
9 *Health-Care Systems/Cumulative Index* (ISBN 0-02-897453-0)

PREFACE

The *Macmillan Health Encyclopedia* is a nine-volume set that explains how the body works; describes the causes and treatment of hundreds of diseases and disorders; provides information on diet and exercise for a healthy lifestyle; discusses key issues in emotional, mental, and sexual health; covers problems relating to the use and abuse of legal and illegal drugs; outlines first-aid procedures; and provides up-to-date information on current health issues.

Written with the support of a distinguished panel of editorial advisors, the encyclopedia puts considerable emphasis on the idea of wellness. It discusses measures an individual can take to prevent illness and provides information about healthy lifestyle choices.

The *Macmillan Health Encyclopedia* is organized topically. Each of the nine volumes relates to an area covered in the school health curriculum. The encyclopedia also supplements course work in biology, psychology, home economics, and physical education. The volumes are organized as follows: 1. *Body Systems: Anatomy and Physiology;* 2. *Communicable Diseases: Symptoms, Diagnosis, Treatment;* 3. *Noncommunicable Diseases and Disorders: Symptoms, Diagnosis, Treatment;* 4. *Nutrition and Fitness;* 5. *Emotional and Mental Health;* 6. *Sexuality and Reproduction;* 7. *Drugs, Alcohol, and Tobacco;* 8. *Safety and Environmental Health;* 9. *Health-Care Systems/Cumulative Index.*

The information in the *Macmillan Health Encyclopedia* is clearly presented and easy to find. Entries are arranged in alphabetical order within each volume. An extensive system of cross-referencing directs the reader from a synonym to the main entry (GERMAN MEASLES see RUBELLA) and from one entry to additional information in other entries. Words printed in SMALL CAPITALS ("These substances, found in a number of NONPRESCRIPTION DRUGS . . .") indicate that there is an entry of that name in the volume. Most entries end with a list of "see also" cross-references to related topics. Entries within the same volume have no number (See also ANTI-INFLAMMATORY DRUGS); entries located in another volume include the volume number (See also HYPERTENSION, 3). All topics covered in a volume can be found in the index at the back of the book. There is also a comprehensive index to the set in Volume 9.

The extensive use of illustration includes colorful drawings, photographs, charts, and graphs to supplement and enrich the information presented in the text.

Questions of particular concern to the reader—When should I see a doctor? What are the risk factors? What can I do to prevent an illness?—are indicated by the following marginal notations: Consult a Physician, Risk Factors, and Healthy Choices.

Although difficult terms are explained within the context of the entry, each volume of the encyclopedia also has its own GLOSSARY. Located in the front of the book, the glossary provides brief definitions of medical or technical terms with which the reader may not be familiar.

A SUPPLEMENTARY SOURCES section at the back of the book contains a listing of suggested reading material, as well as organizations from which additional information can be obtained.

GLOSSARY

acid-base balance The balance maintained by the body between too much and too little acid in body fluids.

addiction The physical or psychological dependence on chemical substances such as alcohol or other drugs; any habit so strong that it cannot be given up easily.

allergy An oversensitivity of the body's immune system to certain substances such as foods, chemicals, pollens, and insect bites that causes formation of antibodies.

amino acids A group of chemical compounds that form the basic structure of proteins. There are nine essential amino acids.

antibody A chemical substance produced by the body in response to an invading microorganism, such as bacteria or viruses. An antibody destroys the foreign substance and removes it from the blood.

antioxidant A chemical compound that prevents oxygen from reacting with other compounds.

autoimmune Pertaining to a disorder caused by the reaction of an individual's immune system to its own body tissue. The body reacts by producing antibodies, the same way it would react to an invading organism.

bacteria (sing. *bacterium*) Single-celled, microscopic organisms, abundant in living things, air, soil, and water. Some are beneficial to humans, while others cause disease (see MICRO-ORGANISMS, 2).

blood pressure The force exerted by blood against the walls of arteries. It is measured when the heart contracts and when it relaxes between contractions.

blood sugar level The concentration of glucose in the bloodstream.

bulimia An eating disorder characterized by binges of eating large amounts of food over a short period of time, often followed by self-induced vomiting.

cardiovascular endurance The ability of the heart, lungs, and blood vessels to carry enough oxygen in order to function efficiently during an extended period of vigorous movement.

catalyst A substance that speeds up a chemical reaction without being changed or destroyed by the action.

colostrum Thick, yellowish fluid, which is rich in antibodies and other protective factors, produced by the mother's breast in the first 2 or 3 days after the birth of a baby. It is replaced by breast milk.

communicable Referring to disease caused by microorganisms or parasites that can be transmitted from one person or animal to another person or animal.

constipation A condition in which bowels are not emptied easily or often enough.

contagious Refers to the time period when an infected person is able to pass an infectious disease to another person by direct or indirect contact; also used to describe the person who is spreading the disease.

edema Any swelling of the body caused by an abnormal accumulation of fluid in spaces between the tissues, organs, or cells.

enzyme A type of protein produced in the cells that causes specific chemical processes that take place in the body. Some enzymes, for example, help break down food.

feces Solid waste material eliminated from the body.

fluoride A mineral useful in helping to prevent tooth decay. It is thought to strengthen the mineral content of tooth enamel and make it more resistant to the acid in foods.

fortified Having the addition of one or more nutrients to a food item that is not normally a good source of the nutrient, such as vitamin D to milk, calcium to orange juice, or certain vitamins to cereals.

free radicals Chemically unstable, oxygen-containing molecules created when food is metabolized or by other environmental influences such as smoking or radiation. They travel through the cells and steal oxygen and other particles from molecules, creating abnormal substances.

gastrointestinal tract The part of the digestive system consisting of the mouth, esophagus, stomach and intestines, and excluding the liver, gallbladder, and pancreas.

genes Structures in cells that are inherited from parents; they help determine an individual's physical and mental characteristics.

glucagon A hormone formed in the pancreas that causes the release of glucose from storage.

glycogen The principle substance for storing carbohydrates in the body. Glycogen is stored in the liver and muscle tissue, changed into glucose, and released into the bloodstream when blood sugar levels fall.

hemoglobin Iron-containing protein found in red blood cells, which transports oxygen from the lungs to the body.

hereditary Passed down from parents to children by means of genes.

hormone A chemical substance, such as insulin or estrogen, that stimulates and regulates certain bodily functions.

hypertension High blood pressure.

infection A condition caused by bacteria, viruses, fungi, or other microorganisms that invade and damage body cells and tissues.

inorganic Made up of or pertaining to matter that is neither animal nor vegetable; not involving living organisms.

insoluble Impossible to dissolve.

insulin A hormone secreted by certain cells of the pancreas that helps the body use sugars and starches.

legume A plant with seeds growing in pods, such as peas, beans, or lentils.

lymphatic system Part of the immune system; a loosely organized system of vessels and ducts that carry lymph fluid from the spaces between cells into the bloodstream.

macromineral Any mineral needed and used by the body in relatively large amounts—such as calcium, potassium, or sodium.

macronutrient Any nutrient the body needs continually in large amounts for essential function—for example, protein, carbohydrates, or fats.

metabolism The physical and chemical processes of the body that convert food into energy and body tissue.

micromineral Any mineral needed and used by the body in very small amounts, such as iron or zinc.

micronutrient A nutrient consisting of vitamins and minerals that the body needs in very small amounts for essential functions.

net weight The weight of a packaged food item exclusive of the weight of the packaging.

opiate Narcotic pain relievers, such as morphine, heroin, and opium.

organic Pertaining to living organisms (plants and animals). Also used to describe a food or nutrient produced without the use of chemical fertilizers, pesticides, or additives.

oxidize To unite with oxygen.

pH balance (potential of Hydrogen) Refers to the acidity or alkalinity of a substance.

physiological Pertaining to the processes, activities, and functions of the body.

processed foods Any food subjected to alteration of texture, mixing with additives, or cooking.

soluble Able to be dissolved.

toxicity The property of being poisonous or the severity of the adverse effects or illness produced by a toxin.

tuber The thick, fleshy part of an underground stem.

vascular Pertaining to the blood vessels and the circulation of blood through the body.

virus The smallest known living infectious agent (see MICROORGANISMS, 2).

▶ AEROBIC DANCE

Aerobic dance is a name for AEROBIC EXERCISE routines that use rhythmic movements set to music to improve respiratory and circulatory function. Aerobic dance can be an excellent way to burn calories and improve *cardiovascular fitness*. One hour of continuous aerobic dancing can burn as much as 600 calories. Aerobic dancing also improves FLEXIBILITY, coordination, and to a lesser degree STRENGTH.

HEALTHY CHOICES

How It Is Done   Aerobic dance is a popular form of EXERCISE, particularly among women. Typically, it is performed in a group, two to three times per week, with an instructor leading the participants. A session usually consists of 5 to 10 minutes of gradual warm-up, followed by 20 to 50 minutes of vigorous exercise, ending with a 5- to 10-minute cool-down. People who cannot attend an aerobics class may purchase videotapes to follow at home.

Aerobic Dance Class. *One of the advantages of aerobic dance for many people is that it enables them to exercise in a social setting.*

HEALTHY CHOICES

Aerobic Dance Safety   If you decide to enter an aerobic dance program, choose one with a duration and intensity that match your level of FITNESS. Also consider the training of the instructor, the hardness of the floor, the frequency of class meetings, and the warm-up and cool-down practices. Wear supportive, well-cushioned shoes that fit well and avoid jarring motions. Aerobic dance must be performed regularly to promote fitness. A workout lasting at least 30 minutes repeated at least three times per week is the minimum for gaining a cardiovascular benefit. (See also ENDURANCE; FITNESS TRAINING; HEART RATE.)

▶ AEROBIC EXERCISE

Aerobic exercise means continuous EXERCISE that can be sustained for long periods of time without causing exhaustion. Examples include RUNNING, WALKING, CYCLING, and SWIMMING. These differ from other energetic activities such as football and gymnastics, which involve periods of effort followed by slack periods during which the body can recover.

ANAEROBIC EXERCISES such as sprinting are also distinct. They involve muscular effort so intense that oxygen is used faster than the lungs and heart can supply it. Anaerobic exercise cannot be sustained.

The Benefits of Aerobic Exercise   Aerobic exercise can provide several health benefits. It is the key to cardiovascular fitness, one of the most important components of physical health. *Cardiovascular fitness* means a strong heart, efficient lungs, and an effective circulatory system.

Regular aerobic workouts increase the strength of the heart muscle so that it can pump more blood with each contraction (beat). This means that although the heart rate still increases during exercise, the average heart rate is lower, putting less strain on your system. The heart does less work to achieve the same level of activity. The heart also recovers from the stress of exercise more quickly, returning to the resting heart rate in a shorter period of time.

Regular aerobic exercise also helps the lungs function better. The amount of air they can take in and breathe out at one time increases. In addition the muscles develop a more extensive network of blood vessels. This allows the blood to transport oxygen and NUTRIENTS with more efficiency to the heart muscle as well as to other muscles of the body.

Aerobic exercise has other important health benefits. It can help keep blood pressure at normal levels and help control weight. It may also raise the blood levels of HDL CHOLESTEROL (the "good" cholesterol) and lower blood sugar levels. Active, fit people have considerably lower death rates from heart disease and cancer than do people who are unfit. Regular aerobic exercise may have psychological benefits as well, including improved self-esteem, reduced anxiety and depression, and an increased ability to deal with stress.

The Limitations of Aerobic Exercise   Although aerobic exercise improves the efficiency of the cardiovascular system, it does not necessarily promote the other components of overall FITNESS, particularly STRENGTH and FLEXIBILITY. Many aerobic activities, such as running and cycling, do little to increase muscle strength and endurance in the upper body, for instance.

HEALTHY CHOICES

HEALTHY CHOICES

Aerobic Exercise.   *Aerobic exercise promotes cardiovascular health, the most important part of fitness.*

To achieve overall fitness, supplement aerobic activities with STRENGTH EXERCISES at least two to three times a week. An efficient way to improve flexibility is to include STRETCHING EXERCISES before and after each aerobic workout.

How to Achieve Aerobic Conditioning Any exercise that raises your heart rate and keeps it there for a prolonged time will help you achieve aerobic conditioning. Many vigorous sports and activities fit this description including AEROBIC DANCE, jumping rope, rowing, cross-country skiing, and racquetball. People with back or knee problems can participate in a type of aerobic activity called *low-impact aerobics* that jars the body less. Low-impact activities include race walking, swimming, and special low-impact dance and exercise routines. A routine of regular brisk walking improves aerobic fitness and includes most of the health benefits of more strenuous programs.

Any amount of aerobic exercise is good for your health and fitness. But to achieve the maximum health benefit, most experts recommend that aerobic exercise be performed continuously for a minimum of 20 to 30 minutes three times a week. To increase conditioning or speed weight loss, a person should exercise more frequently and for longer periods. Hard workouts should be alternated each day with less demanding sessions so that muscles will not be overtaxed.

To promote optimum cardiovascular fitness through aerobic exercise, you can seek to maintain your HEART RATE within a target range. Your target range runs from 60 to 75 percent of your maximum heart rate (which can be estimated as 220 minus your age in years). The pulse should be checked several times during an aerobic exercise session to make sure the heart rate is within these limits.

Aerobic exercise should be preceded by a warm-up period. This allows for a maximal effort. Every session should end with a cool-down, a time of light activity, to let the heart rate gradually return to normal. If you neglect the cool-down, you may feel light-headed or dizzy.

Anyone participating in a strenuous physical activity should be alert to signs that the activity should be discontinued. Stop exercising if symptoms of unusual breathlessness, nausea, or dizziness occur. Acute chest pain or pressure, or pain radiating through the shoulder or arm for more than 2 minutes, may be very serious; medical help should be summoned immediately. (See also ENDURANCE; FITNESS TRAINING; SPORTS AND FITNESS.)

► **AGRICULTURAL CHEMICALS** Agricultural chemicals are substances used by farmers to improve the quantity and quality of the foods they produce. These chemicals work in a variety of ways and include fertilizers, pesticides, and growth regulators.

Fertilizers Fertilizers are used to provide essential nutrients that plants need to grow. "Organic" fertilizers consist of decomposed plant material and manure. "Chemical" fertilizers are usually manufactured, primarily in the form of inorganic salts. Both types of fertilizers deliver the same basic nutrients to the soil.

Pesticides   Pesticides are chemicals that are applied to crops to control attacks by insects, fungi, rodents, and competing plants and weeds. Pesticides are poisons—the *-cide* ending means "killer." Ideally, they should do their job and then break down into harmless substances before the food is eaten. In reality, traces of poisons can remain on fruits and vegetables right to the consumer's table, which is why it is a good idea to wash all produce before eating. If you see discoloration or strange markings on a fruit or vegetable, discard it. If you become severely ill after eating a fruit or vegetable, get medical attention promptly.

CONSULT A
PHYSICIAN

Growth Regulators   Growth regulators are used to enhance the growth and size of both plants and animals. They do so by artificially mimicking natural substances called *hormones*. In plants they typically have no residual effect on the resulting food products. Their use in meat production is considerably more controversial. Controlled use of growth stimulants is currently allowed in meats and poultry marketed for the United States but is prohibited by many European countries. (See also FOOD ADDITIVES; FOOD SAFETY.)

► ANAEROBIC EXERCISE
Anaerobic exercise is exercise that demands more oxygen from the body than it can supply. It is intense EXERCISE, such as weight lifting or sprinting, that lasts for only a short period of time. During anaerobic exercise, oxygen is quickly used up, and lactic acid (a byproduct of muscle use) builds up in the muscles. The result is an *oxygen debt* in the muscles. For the muscles to return to normal, the lactic acid must combine with new oxygen to repay the oxygen debt when the exercise is over.

Anaerobic Exercise.   *Trained as well as untrained individuals may suffer from uncomfortable symptoms immediately after strenuous anaerobic exercise.*

HEALTHY CHOICES

Results of Anaerobic Exercise   After an anaerobic activity, most people continue to breathe deeply and rapidly in order to get more oxygen to the muscle cells that need it. Extreme anaerobic activity may also produce headache, blurry vision, nausea, vomiting, or light-headedness. The result of a buildup of lactic acid, these symptoms, although uncomfortable, are not serious. When they occur, a person should keep moving or walking until they subside. Full recovery can take 1 or 2 hours, depending on the extent of the oxygen debt (although most people feel better within a few minutes).

The Role of Anaerobic Exercise in a Fitness Program   Anaerobic exercise is not advisable for people starting a fitness program. AEROBIC EXERCISE is a better choice because it puts less stress on the body while improving cardiovascular health.

Anaerobic exercise can be part of a well-conditioned athlete's fitness program because the heart and circulatory system are already well conditioned. This type of exercise can help develop both STRENGTH and muscular and cardiovascular ENDURANCE. Weight lifting, for example, helps develop strong muscles. However, aerobic exercise is recommended in all fitness programs because anaerobic exercise offers little cardiovascular benefit. (See also FITNESS; FITNESS TRAINING; STRENGTH EXERCISE.)

▶ ANOREXIA NERVOSA   see EATING DISORDERS

▶ APPETITE

Appetite is a healthy desire for food. It is a pleasant sensation people feel in anticipation of eating.

Appetite should not be confused with hunger. Appetite is a learned response; *hunger* is a physiological response to the need for food. Hunger is often unpleasant and sometimes painful. The feelings of appetite, hunger, and *satiety* (feeling full) work together to regulate eating behaviors in ways that are not fully understood.

Both physical and psychological factors can cause people to lose their appetite. Illness or emotional upset may cause a temporary loss of appetite. Psychological disorders like depression may result in a persistent loss of appetite. For example, *anorexia nervosa,* a serious psychological condition marked by an irrational fear of gaining weight, causes a suppression of appetite.

The appetite can also increase for physical and psychological reasons. For instance, an *overactive thyroid* gland increases energy requirements and stimulates a person's appetite. The smell, taste, or appearance of food may also spur a person's appetite, as may an increased level of exercise.

RISK FACTORS

Some people use drugs called *appetite suppressants* to lose weight. These drugs work by decreasing a person's appetite and should be used only for a short time and under a physician's supervision. Prolonged use can cause dangerous side effects and lead to addiction and is generally not effective for weight loss. (See also DIETS; EATING DISORDERS; FOOD CRAVING; HUNGER; WEIGHT MANAGEMENT; THYROID DISORDERS, 3; ANOREXIA/ BULIMIA, 5.)

▶ ARTIFICIAL SWEETENERS

Artificial sweeteners are synthetic substances used in place of SUGAR to sweeten foods and drinks. They are found in powdered table-sugar substitutes and in processed foods and drinks. Artificial sweeteners taste like sugar but have few or no CALORIES, which is why they are helpful to people on reducing diets. They have little or no nutritional value. The three best-known artificial sweeteners are *saccharin, cyclamate,* and *aspartame.*

Saccharin Saccharin, first introduced at the end of the nineteenth century, is used in many products, especially soft drinks, and as a powdered sugar substitute (Sweet 'n Low). In the late 1970s, its safety was challenged when scientists identified a possible link between saccharin and tumors in laboratory rats. Although the Food and Drug Administration considered banning the product, extensive studies have failed to demonstrate that saccharin causes cancer in humans. In the United States,

RISK FACTORS
▶ ▶ ▶ ▶ ▶ ▶

Aspartame. *Although aspartame is safe when used moderately, people with an inherited disorder called phenylketonuria are advised to limit their intake of this sweetener.*

however, all products containing saccharin must now include a warning label. Its use is banned in Canada, except by prescription.

Cyclamate   Cyclamate, introduced in the 1950s, was widely used as a sweetener until 1970, when it was banned from the American market because of a possible link to cancer in laboratory animals. Its use remains legal in Canada.

Aspartame   Introduced in 1981, aspartame, known most commonly to consumers as NutraSweet®, is used in soft drinks, chewing gum, and cereal, among other foods. It is also the main ingredient in Equal, a powdered substitute for sugar. Roughly 200 times sweeter than *sucrose*, aspartame results from the chemical marriage of two amino acids, neither of which is itself sweet. Aspartame is believed to be safe when consumed in reasonable amounts. Today it is by far the most popular artificial sweetener in the United States. (See also DIET FOOD.)

▶ ATHLETIC FOOTWEAR

Athletic footwear includes specially constructed shoes designed to protect the foot and maximize performance during sports activities. Today people can choose from many kinds of athletic footwear designed for specific sports, including running, tennis, basketball, aerobics, and walking.

Types of Footwear   Athletic footwear designed for different sports differs in the thickness and rigidity of the shoe's sole, the height of the ankle collar, the amount and placement of cushioning, the construction of the heel, and a variety of other features. But in general there are two classes of athletic footwear. One type is designed for activities that involve primarily forward motion, such as running and walking. The second type is for activities that involve a lot of sudden stopping, starting, and lateral motion, such as tennis and aerobic dance. These types of shoes are reinforced under the toe and have sturdier sides than do running shoes. As a result, they also tend to be a bit heavier.

Proper Footwear. *Sports that involve mostly forward motion (such as running) require different footwear than do sports that involve stops, starts, and movements from side to side (such as tennis).*

Orthotic Devices When some people run, their feet tend to roll inward (*pronation*) or outward (*supination*), putting additional stress on the knees, hips, back, and ankles. When the rolling is severe or causes recurring pain, doctors who specialize in foot problems may prescribe orthotic devices, or orthoses. These custom-made devices of foam, leather, or plastic fit inside the wearer's running shoes. The orthotic devices correct improper foot motion and make sports activities easier and more comfortable.

Purchasing Footwear It is not necessary to purchase a separate pair of athletic shoes for each kind of sports activity. Running shoes are best for running, but tennis or basketball shoes can be worn for many other kinds of sports, including aerobic dance, racquetball, and volleyball. Many people find that high-topped shoes help to support the ankle and prevent the foot from rolling over.

Athletic shoes can be expensive and should be chosen with care to prevent discomfort and injury. Choose footwear that fits well and feels comfortable. Even top-quality athletic shoes lose their ability to absorb shocks over time. Replace shoes when they become worn.

▶ BETA CAROTENE

Beta carotene is a NUTRIENT found in many vegetables and fruits that the body converts to VITAMIN A. Once converted, it performs all the functions of vitamin A, which include promoting normal development of bones and teeth, maintaining healthy cell structure in the skin and mucous membranes, and aiding normal vision.

Beta carotene may have additional benefits as an antioxidant. An *antioxidant* is a substance that helps the body fight *free radicals,* unstable molecules that can damage cells. Free radicals form in the body during normal metabolism through exposure to various damaging external factors such as X rays, cigarette smoke, alcohol, or pollutants. The antioxidant activity of beta carotene may play a role in preventing cancer and heart disease and may help strengthen the immune system. Further studies are needed, however, before these findings are proved conclusively.

HEALTHY CHOICES

Good sources of beta carotene are carrots, sweet potatoes, winter squash, kale, broccoli, spinach, apricots, and cantaloupe. The National Cancer Institute and the U.S. Department of Agriculture recommend five $1/2$-cup (118 mL) servings of such nutrient-rich fruits and vegetables each day, which would supply 5 to 6 grams of beta carotene. (See also VITAMINS.)

▶ BEVERAGES

Beverages are drinks consumed to meet the body's need for WATER and NUTRIENTS. Nutrition experts recommend drinking at least eight glasses of water or some other healthy beverage a day—more during periods of exercise or hot weather. An adequate beverage intake helps maintain good

Varied Nutritional Value of Beverages. *Fruit juices are much more nutritious than are sodas and fruit-flavored drinks.*

health and prevents DEHYDRATION, a condition in which the body's water level becomes dangerously low. The nutritional value of beverages varies, however (see illustration: Varied Nutritional Value of Beverages). Milk and fruit juice, for example, offer valuable nutrients, whereas soft drinks are very low in nutrients and can be high in CALORIES.

HEALTHY CHOICES

Water   Water is essential to good health. It is the best fluid to drink when exercising, better even than specially formulated "sports drinks." Some people believe bottled water is superior to or safer than tap water, but studies have shown that this is not necessarily true. The mineral content of any water is not nutritionally significant. However, the fluoride added to many community water supplies provides a health bonus by helping to prevent tooth decay.

Soft Drinks   Soft drinks are America's most popular beverage, especially among people aged 12 to 34. The average consumption is more than 16 ounces (about 500 mL) per person per day. Although many are sugar-free and caffeine-free, soft drinks are still the leading source of added SUGAR in the American diet and the second leading source of *caffeine*, a stimulant legally classified as a drug. Regular soft drinks contain between 9 and 12 teaspoons of sugar, which equals 144 to 192 calories in each 12-ounce (355-mL) can. Diet soft drinks use ARTIFICIAL SWEETENERS such as saccharin or aspartame (NutraSweet®) in place of sugar. The nutritional value of soft drinks is extremely low, which is why they are often said to provide "empty" calories. Although a moderate intake of soft drinks should pose no health problems, nutritionists recommend that they should not take the place of more nutritious beverages in the diet (especially milk for young children).

HEALTHY CHOICES

Fruit Drinks   Fruit drinks and juices can be a healthy alternative to soft drinks, although their nutritional content varies. Reading labels carefully will help in selecting the most nutritious type of fruit drink. Fresh or frozen 100 percent fruit juices are generally most nutritious. A cup of orange juice, for example, provides 1.8 grams of protein, essential VITA-MINS and MINERALS, and just 88 calories. A flavored fruit drink, on the other hand, may contain only 10 percent natural fruit juices.

Milk   Milk is a nutritious beverage. Young children need to drink milk (if they are not allergic) to obtain the necessary calcium for strong bones and teeth. A cup of milk provides almost 9 grams of protein, assorted vit-amins (including A, C, and D), calcium, iron, and 159 calories. A cup of skim milk, which has nearly all naturally occurring FATS removed, is a low-calorie alternative to whole milk, with 89 calories and all the essen-tial vitamins and minerals.

Tea and Coffee   Tea and coffee, when prepared without cream, sugar, or other additives, have scarcely any calories and no significant food value. Both beverages naturally contain caffeine, although they are avail-able in decaffeinated forms. (See also CAFFEINE, 7.)

▶ **BODY BUILDING**   Body building is a sport that uses variations of WEIGHT TRAINING to increase muscle mass. The goal is a well-defined, highly muscled, and symmetrical body. This activity is becoming more popular among both men and women, and as a professional sport, competitions include cash prizes.

The goal of body building differs from that of weight training. Weight-training programs aim to develop muscle tone and STRENGTH,

Body-Building Competition.
In professional competitions, judges evaluate the body builders' muscle definition, shape, and size as well as overall body proportions.

while body building has more to do with the aesthetics of muscle definition and form.

The Regimen for Body Building This sport requires intense, specialized techniques using free weights or resistance machines. Hours of daily effort are necessary to achieve and maintain the desired muscle size and definition. Changing one's BODY COMPOSITION is an important part of body building, with very low body fat considered desirable. Diet consequently is a crucial part of a body builder's training program.

RISK FACTORS
▶ ▶ ▶ ▶ ▶ ▶

The Risks of Body Building Like all sports involving weights, body building does little to develop cardiovascular fitness. In addition, body builders sometimes lose muscle FLEXIBILITY as they add muscle mass. To achieve total FITNESS, a body builder must include flexibility exercises and AEROBIC EXERCISES. The use of *anabolic steroids* among body builders is widespread. Many participants are tempted to take these potentially harmful drugs because they help build muscle bulk. Because the possible side effects of anabolic steroids include harmful physical and emotional changes, these drugs should be avoided. (See also ANAEROBIC EXERCISE; STRENGTH EXERCISE; STEROIDS, 7.)

▶ **BODY COMPOSITION**   Body composition refers to the proportions of the major components of the body and, in particular, to the ratio of the body's lean tissue to fat tissue. Body composition is usually expressed as the percentage of body weight that is fat.

Body Fat The body needs a certain amount of fat for survival. It is essential for storing certain NUTRIENTS and converting them into energy, providing insulation for the body, and protecting internal organs. On the

RISK FACTORS
▶ ▶ ▶ ▶ ▶ ▶

other hand, too much BODY FAT is unhealthy. Excess fat increases the risk of many diseases, including heart disease, cardiovascular disease, high blood pressure, diabetes, and certain cancers. The location of excess fat is also important: Fat around the abdomen represents a greater health risk than does fat elsewhere on the body.

Although too much body fat is a health concern, ideas about "ideal" body composition are complicated by cultural and personal factors as well. In America, fashion often decrees unrealistically low body-fat levels, especially for women. In reality, ideal body composition differs greatly from person to person (see illustration: Body Types). The appropriate proportion of body fat is one consistent with optimal health over the lifespan. In general, the acceptable range for men is between 12 and 25 percent of total weight; for women, it is between 22 and 35 percent. People at or above the top of these ranges are generally considered OVERWEIGHT for health reasons and should start a WEIGHT MANAGEMENT program that includes a healthy diet and regular, progressive exercise. (See also EATING DISORDERS.)

Exercise that develops cardiovascular FITNESS can help change body composition. With exercise, the percentage of fat tissue decreases, and the percentage of lean tissue increases.

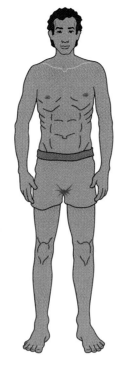 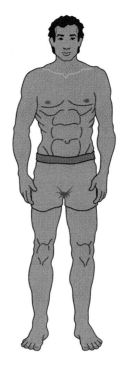 

Body Types. *Hereditary factors have a great deal to do with a person's body composition, which is also affected by diet and fitness level. Three examples of the wide variety of body types are shown here: tall and thin (left), average height and muscular (center), and short and stocky (right).*

Measuring Body Composition   One common measure for estimating body composition is the *body-mass index* (BMI), the ratio of weight (in kilograms) divided by height (in meters) squared. A BMI of 27 is the upper end of the range of body-fat level recommended by the U.S. Surgeon General. Other techniques for measuring body composition include the *fatfold* (or skinfold) *test, hydrostatic* (or underwater) *weighing,* and *electric conductivity* (or bioelectrical impedance). (See also DIETS; OBESITY; WEIGHT ASSESSMENT.)

▶ **BODY FAT**

The scientific name given to fats and closely related substances is *lipids*. Lipids are vital chemicals in the body, performing many different and essential functions. However, too much body fat is associated with several causes of early death.

Functions of Lipids   There are different kinds of lipids, and they are important for many body processes. Lipids are a basic substance in all body cells and are necessary for the body to make use of some minerals and vitamins. Some lipids play a key part in producing hormones, which regulate body processes. Others are vital for the formation of blood clots. And an important type of lipid called *fatty acids* is used for energy storage and production.

Energy can be produced for the body by three different substances: *amino acids*, which are also the building blocks of PROTEIN; GLUCOSE, the body's working carbohydrate; and lipids. Of these, amino acids are the least desirable energy source because using them for energy causes significant damage—they exist only in functioning tissues of the body such as muscle.

Glucose, while it is the most complete energy source, has only limited storage areas. It is saved as glycogen in the liver and to some extent in the muscles themselves. However, lipids have virtually unlimited storage, within expandable *fat cells*. In fact, excess amino acids and glucose in the diet are often metabolized into storable lipids—and they cannot be changed back.

The fat cells of the body serve other useful functions besides energy storage. They provide heat insulation under the skin and safety cushioning around the vital organs. But their major function is to be the reserve storehouse for the body's energy, releasing lipids to provide physical energy when it is needed. And the storage they provide is very efficient: 1 gram of lipids can produce 9 CALORIES of energy, compared to only 4 calories from a gram of glucose or of amino acids.

RISK FACTORS
▶ ▶ ▶ ▶ ▶ ▶

Lipids, Heart Disease, and Other Problems   Though lipids play many important roles in the body, excessive amounts of them, whether in the form of body fat or fatty acids in the blood, can seriously stress the cardiovascular system. Extra body fat forces the heart to work harder to nourish the additional living tissue. It can also contribute to the development of problems related to CHOLESTEROL, including atherosclerosis, heart attacks, and strokes.

HEALTHY CHOICES
▪▪▪▪▪▪▪▪▪▪▪▪

Because of the various health problems associated with being overweight, medical experts recommend that only 12 to 25 percent of a man's weight should be in the form of body fat. For women, this number should be 22 to 35 percent. People who exceed these percentages should use more energy by getting regular EXERCISE, and they should also cut back on eating fatty foods. The same advice applies to people who have excessively high lipid levels in the blood. (See also BODY COMPOSITION; ENERGY, FOOD; FATS; FATS, OILS, AND SWEETS GROUP; RISK FACTORS; ATHEROSCLEROSIS, **3**; HEART DISEASE, **3**.)

▶ **BODY METABOLISM**   Body metabolism includes all the biochemical changes that occur in the body to meet energy needs and to repair and replace tissues. Metabolism consists of two processes, anabolism and catabolism. In *anabolism,* the simple products of DIGESTION are combined to form more complex substances. These substances are used by the body to grow, to repair body tissues, and to store energy. In *catabolism,* digested NUTRIENTS are further broken down to produce heat and energy. These processes are controlled by *hormones* and take place continuously in the body.

Measuring Metabolism   Basal metabolic rate is a measurement of the minimum amount of energy, counted in CALORIES, needed to maintain vital body processes, including circulation, breathing, and body temperature. It is measured while a person is at complete rest but not sleeping. The basal metabolic rate varies from person to person, depending on age, weight, and level of fitness. Men typically have higher rates than do women.

Physical Activity and Metabolic Rate. *Exercise increases overall metabolic rate. A person who is in good shape burns calories at a faster rate than someone who rarely exercises.*

The number of calories needed every day to support basal metabolism is surprisingly high—approximately 50 to 70 percent of calories consumed are used to sustain the basic work of cells. The remaining calories are used for all voluntary activities, including exercise and sports. Any unused calories are stored as fat.

Factors Affecting Basal Metabolism Many factors affect basal metabolic rate. Hormones secreted from the thyroid and adrenal glands have the most influence on the basal metabolic rate. An increase of hormones from either gland will raise body metabolism. For example, a surge of adrenaline, secreted by the adrenal glands in response to emotions such as anger or fear, will stimulate metabolism for a short period.

Both body temperature and environmental temperature also affect basal metabolic rate. A rise in body temperature of 1°F (0.55°C) increases basal metabolism about 7 percent, so a person with a fever will have increased energy needs. When the temperature of the air drops and a person does not put on extra clothes to slow the rate of heat loss, the body will increase its basal metabolic rate to produce more heat. Age also affects metabolic rate. It is higher in infancy and during puberty and generally slows with age.

Metabolism and Weight Management Some researchers believe that people may have a given weight range, or set-point, that is natural for their body. According to this theory, the body alters its basal metabolic rate to maintain weight at that particular set-point. For example, if someone with a high set-point weight tries to lose weight by strict dieting, the body responds by burning calories more slowly and efficiently (thus slowing metabolism) to maintain a stable weight. This theory has not yet been proved, but if it is true, it may help explain why dieting is so difficult for most individuals. The set-point theory does not mean, however, that losing weight is impossible. Increased physical activity is another important factor that raises the body's overall metabolic rate, including some increase in basal metabolic rate.

Metabolism and Fitness   All body tissues constantly undergo breakdown and repair, and some have greater basal energy needs than do others. The brain, major organs, and muscles require relatively larger amounts of energy in the form of calories. Bones and fat require less. A person who is in good shape usually has more muscle tissue than has someone who rarely exercises and will therefore burn calories at a faster rate. The key to controlling metabolic rate, then, is exercise. Understanding this relationship may help people meet WEIGHT MANAGEMENT goals and plan sensible long-range fitness programs. (See also AEROBIC EXERCISE; ENERGY, FOOD; ENERGY, PHYSICAL; EXERCISE; REST; METABOLISM, **1**.)

HEALTHY CHOICES

▶ BREADS AND CEREALS GROUP   The breads and cereals food group is a class of foods made from grains such as wheat, rice, oats, and corn. In some FOOD GROUP SYSTEMS, this category of foods is called *grains;* in others, *breads, cereals, pasta, and rice.* Breads and cereals are especially rich in desirable NUTRIENTS such as complex CARBOHYDRATES and PROTEINS and low in FATS and CALORIES. Many breads and cereals also contain important amounts of VITAMINS, MINERALS, and FIBER.

Nutrition from Breads and Cereals   The breads and cereals group includes a number of different foods.

- *Breads* may be made from many grains, including wheat, corn, rye, and oats. *Yeast breads,* such as white and whole-wheat loaves, are made with yeast. *Yeast* is a tiny plant that, when combined with other ingredients, causes bread to rise. *Quick breads,* such as muffins and corn bread, rise through the action of baking powder or other ingredients. *Flat breads,* which include tortillas and pita bread, do not rise. White bread and many types of rolls are made from white processed flour. During processing many important nutrients, especially B vitamins and IRON, are lost. Breads to which nutrients have been added are called *enriched breads.* *Whole-grain breads* are those in which unrefined grains have been used and important nutrients have therefore not been lost. Whole-grain breads also contain *bran,* a part of the grain that provides both nutrients and fiber.
- *Cereals* are breakfast foods made from grains. Some are ready to eat, and others require cooking. As with white flour, the processing that many cereals go through depletes them of nutrients. *Fortified cereals* are ones to which nutrients have been added. Choosing whole-grain and fortified cereals is the best way to ensure good nutrition from these foods.
- *Rice* is also a cereal grain. The outer coverings of *white rice,* the hull and the bran, have been removed. Because these coverings

Breads and Cereals.

include so many nutrients, most white rice is enriched with added vitamins. *Brown rice* has had the hull removed but retains the fiber-rich bran. This makes it more flavorful and more nutritious. Using the proper amount of water when cooking rice is important to retain the rice's full nutritive value.

▸ *Pasta* is another member of the breads and cereals group. Spaghetti, macaroni, and noodles are all types of pasta. Many kinds are made from a type of wheat flour called semolina. Pasta dough can be cut into dozens of shapes and may be bought fresh or dried. Pasta may also be enriched with vitamins. It should always be cooked according to the package directions, using the correct amount of water. Pasta should never be rinsed after cooking it, since rinsing can wash away important nutrients.

Daily Servings of Breads and Cereals Most food-group systems suggest making foods from the breads and cereals group the largest single part of your daily diet, recommending four or more servings for teenagers and young adults. Whenever possible, you should choose whole-grain breads and cereals rather than processed ones, which can have large amounts of sugar and salt added to them. (See also EXCHANGE SYSTEM; FATS, OILS, AND SWEETS GROUP; FIVE FOOD GROUPS SYSTEM; FOOD PYRAMID SYSTEM; FOUR FOOD GROUPS SYSTEM; FRUITS AND VEGETABLES GROUP; MEATS, EGGS, AND LEGUMES GROUP; MILK AND MILK PRODUCTS GROUP; STARCH.)

HEALTHY CHOICES

▸ BREAST MILK

HEALTHY CHOICES

Breast-feeding.

Breast milk is milk that is produced in a woman's *mammary glands* after she has given birth. It is the most complete food for babies. It provides virtually all the NUTRIENTS an infant needs as well as *antibodies* that protect the child from diseases. Breast milk also stimulates the development of the infant's gastrointestinal tract.

Breast milk provides about 600 CALORIES of food energy per day to the infant. It is a mix of CARBOHYDRATES, FATS, and PROTEIN that promotes an infant's proper growth and development. Breast milk also provides nearly all the VITAMINS, MINERALS, and WATER an infant needs. VITAMIN D, fluoride, and IRON are the only essential nutrients infants cannot obtain from breast milk.

A new mother usually does not produce milk until the third day after her child's birth. Until then, the breasts produce *colostrum,* a fatty substance containing white blood cells and antibodies from the mother's bloodstream that help protect the infant against bacterial infection and viruses such as colds.

Many pediatricians and family physicians recommend breast-feeding. In addition to providing valuable antibodies and essential nutrients, breast-feeding involves a physical closeness that strengthens the bond between mother and child. However, it is not recommended for a mother who is taking certain medications, who is a drug addict or alcoholic, or who has certain communicable diseases, such as tuberculosis or hepatitis. (See also ANTIBODY, **2**; BREAST, **6**.)

▶ **BULIMIA**   **see** EATING DISORDERS

▶ **CALCIUM**

Calcium is the most plentiful MINERAL in the human body. It plays an important role in a number of bodily functions, including blood clotting, muscle contraction, the transmission of nerve impulses, and the manufacture and maintenance of bones and teeth. Calcium-rich foods include milk and milk products such as yogurt, cheese, and ice cream; green vegetables such as broccoli, spinach, and collard greens; and fish and shellfish such as salmon, oysters, and sardines with bones.

Most of the calcium in the body is contained in the bones in the form of *calcium phosphate*. The remainder is found in the blood and other body fluids. The amount of calcium in the body is controlled by the actions of certain *hormones* and VITAMIN D. When the level of calcium in the blood is too low, the blood absorbs more from the intestines or bones.

Calcium Deficiency   Adequate amounts of calcium in the diet are important for the formation of teeth and bones in children. An inadequate amount of calcium in the diet can result in bone degeneration and crippling deformities. Children and adolescents whose diets are deficient in calcium may develop *rickets*, a condition causing softening of the bones and bowing of the legs. Adults may be prone to *osteoporosis*, a condition in which the bones lose calcium and become brittle and porous. Although almost everyone suffers loss of bone mass after the age of 35, osteoporosis is more common in women following *menopause*.

Sampling of Foods Rich in Calcium.   *The recommended dietary allowance for calcium is 700 to 800 mg per day. Pregnant women and women over the age of 50 should consume as much as 1,500 mg per day. Foods rich in this mineral include sardines with bones, nonfat milk or yogurt, shrimp, and spinach.*

HEALTHY CHOICES
●●●●●●●●●●●●

Most experts advise that men and women continue to eat calcium-rich foods throughout their lives in order to maintain adequate stores of calcium in the body. Certain factors affect the body's ability to absorb calcium. Increased levels of vitamin D, phosphorus, and lactose (milk sugar) in the diet will aid the absorption of calcium. Too much protein in the diet can limit absorption. (See also VITAMINS; OSTEOPOROSIS, 3.)

▶ CALORIE

A calorie is a unit of heat energy. It is used to measure both stored energy (as in food) and energy expended (as by any living organism). In relation to nutrition, *calorie* generally refers to a unit of energy that is, technically speaking, a *kilocalorie*. This is the amount of heat needed to raise the temperature of 1 kilogram of water 1°C.

Calories are an important concept to understand in relation to diet. Your body needs enough of them in the form of food to provide adequate fuel for all of its energy expenditures. When you consume too many calories over a period of time, your body stores the excess, primarily in the form of fat, causing you to gain weight. When you burn more calories than you consume, you lose weight because fat cells are reduced in size as their fat is consumed to provide energy.

A constant body weight results from a long-term balance of calories consumed (energy intake) and calories burned (energy expenditure), a concept called the *energy-balance equation*. An average adult burns between 1,500 and 3,000 calories a day. This number varies owing to a wide range of factors, including age, sex, weight, activity level, and rate of BODY METABOLISM.

> When you consume too many calories over a period of time, your body stores the excess, primarily in the form of fat, causing you to gain weight.

Calories and Energy Intake The energy values of specific foods are measured by determining how many calories they contain. This is done in a laboratory with a device called a *bomb calorimeter* in which small quantities of foods are burned. The heat they generate is then measured in terms of calories.

Using this method, nutritionists have counted the calories contained in every imaginable kind of food. A teaspoon of sugar, for example, has 16 calories, a glass of whole milk has 150, and a 3-ounce (85-g) hamburger patty has 245. Calorie counts such as these are widely available in diet and nutrition books, in many cookbooks, and on many food packages. They can be used to determine how many calories you are consuming daily.

Calories and Energy Expenditure In similar ways, researchers have calculated how many calories are burned in the course of specific human activities. Basically, the more a body has to work, the more fuel it requires in the form of calories. The level of physical activity, or EXERCISE, is therefore one of the largest variables in a person's daily energy expenditure.

Every physical activity burns calories at its own rate. For example, a 150-pound (68-kg) person burns roughly 320 calories an hour walking (at 3 miles per hour), 400 calories an hour playing tennis (singles), 750 calories an hour jumping rope, and 1,280 calories an hour running (at 10 miles per hour). The more strenuous the activity, the more calories it requires.

Balancing Intake and Expenditure   Understanding the calorie values of foods and of exercise is critical to anyone concerned with WEIGHT MANAGEMENT. The essential fact is that every 3,500 calories you consume in excess of what you expend is converted to 1 pound of body-fat tissue. Thus, to lose 10 pounds (4.5 kg), you would have to burn 35,000 (3,500 × 10) calories more than you consume over a period of time.

Although that figure seems high, even minor adjustments to eating and exercise can produce large shifts in the energy-balance equation. For example, reducing calorie consumption by just 100 calories a day combined with just 3 hours of moderate exercise a week can produce a weight loss of 20 to 30 pounds in a year. (See also DIETS; ENERGY, FOOD; ENERGY, PHYSICAL; WEIGHT-GAIN STRATEGY; WEIGHT-LOSS STRATEGY; METABOLISM, 1.)

▶ **CARBOHYDRATES**   Carbohydrates are one of the three main groups of *macronutrients*, nutrients that the body needs in large amounts. They are compounds of carbon, hydrogen, and oxygen atoms that are formed in quantity within all plants. People have limited capacity to store carbohydrates, however; what cannot be used or held in the liver or the muscles tends to be turned into fat.

Carbohydrates perform four main functions, three of which are connected with energy. They are the most important source of energy for all body functions; they are necessary to allow efficient use of FATS as an energy source; and they protect PROTEINS from being used for energy in emergencies. Finally, in the form of fiber, they provide bulk needed to aid digestion.

Complex Carbohydrates   Depending on their chemical structures, carbohydrates are either complex or simple. Complex carbohydrates are large molecules with many carbon atoms: The most complex of all, STARCHES, have about 200,000 per molecule. Foods rich in starch molecules include breads, pasta, potatoes, and rice. They usually take time to digest, and they contain many other valuable substances as well: for example, VITAMINS, MINERALS, and proteins. They also typically contain much water and fiber.

Like starch, FIBER is a complex carbohydrate found in most foods of plant origin. Unlike starch, however, fiber cannot be digested by humans. Instead, it provides roughage that binds with solid wastes and aids in their elimination from the body.

Simple Carbohydrates   Simple carbohydrates are sugars, with as few as 6 carbon atoms per molecule. Once again, they are present in many valuable plant foods, especially fruits, berries, and certain root crops. However, sugary foods also include foods made with refined sugar, and these foods are often very high in CALORIES for their weight. They are easy to digest and provide quick energy, but if consumed in large amounts, they are particularly likely to be converted into body fat.

RISK FACTORS
▶ ▶ ▶ ▶ ▶ ▶

Complex and Simple Carbohydrates. *Complex carbohydrates are found in bread, rice, potatoes, and pasta. These foods have more nutritional value than do the simple-carbohydrate foods made with refined sugar.*

HEALTHY CHOICES

RISK FACTORS
▶ ▶ ▶ ▶ ▶ ▶

Carbohydrates in the Diet   A diet high in complex carbohydrates can be both satisfying and nutritionally beneficial for weight-conscious people and for athletes. Athletes in particular have found it helpful to eat a diet rich in complex carbohydrates for several days before an athletic event. This has proved a reliable way to create energy reserves in muscles and thus extend the time that the body is able to maintain strenuous activity.

Eating simple-carbohydrate foods such as candy bars provides a quick burst of energy, but it is short-lived and often followed by an energy slump. And there can be additional negative effects. Sugars play an indirect role in tooth decay by adhering to teeth and gums and providing a good environment for bacteria. Sugars also pose potential problems for people with diabetes, who lack the ability to regulate the amount of sugar in their blood.

Most Americans do not consume enough complex carbohydrates. In 1977 the U.S. Senate Select Committee on Nutrition and Human Needs recommended that 60 percent of total daily calories come from carbohydrates, with no more than 15 percent of this amount from simple sugars. Sports nutritionists have refined this advice and suggested that endurance athletes raise their carbohydrate level to 70 percent. (See also BREADS AND CEREALS GROUP; ENERGY, FOOD; NUTRIENTS.)

▶ **CHOLESTEROL**   Cholesterol is a waxlike, fat-related substance that is an important part of all animal cells. Among its many roles, cholesterol helps produce *bile,* which aids in digestion. Cholesterol is also involved in creating certain *hormones,* VITAMIN D, and the outer coverings that protect nerve fibers. Most cholesterol is manufactured by the liver, but cholesterol is also present in foods of animal origin, such as butter, eggs, meats, and cheeses.

RISK FACTORS

Cholesterol in the Blood   Although it is essential to life, when too much cholesterol circulates in the blood it can increase the risk of certain diseases. Studies have linked diets high in saturated FATS and cholesterol to *atherosclerosis,* an accumulation of cholesterol in the inner walls of arteries. Atherosclerosis can lead to stroke, coronary artery disease, and heart attack. (See also ATHEROSCLEROSIS, **3;** HEART DISEASE, **3.**)

Cholesterol is carried through the bloodstream by special molecules called *lipoproteins.* Two major types of lipoproteins are important cholesterol carriers. They are differentiated by their size and density. The larger is *low-density lipoprotein,* or LDL. It is associated with increased risk of atherosclerosis. For this reason, the cholesterol that LDL carries is referred to as "bad" cholesterol. Smaller and denser, *high-density lipoprotein,* or HDL, appears to carry excess cholesterol away from the artery walls and back to the liver, where it is processed and excreted. Because HDL performs a kind of cleanup function, its cholesterol is referred to as "good" cholesterol.

Cholesterol Levels   There are two types of blood tests that measure cholesterol levels. The simplest (and least expensive) measures the total amount of cholesterol being carried within the blood. Fewer than 200 milligrams per deciliter (mg/dL) is usually considered to be healthy, while 240 mg/dL or more is considered a high cholesterol level. This test makes no distinction between good and bad cholesterol, however.

The second test provides a "cholesterol profile," measuring how much cholesterol is carried by LDLs and how much by HDLs. This yields a "cholesterol ratio," for example, 130/30 or 4.3. Doctors usually consider the results of both tests before they decide on any treatment: A high HDL measure (which causes a low ratio) is a good sign and makes a high figure on the first test less worrisome.

RISK FACTORS

Controlling Cholesterol Problems   A variety of factors influence levels of cholesterol in the blood. The most important factor is diet, but heredity (a family history of cholesterol), diseases such as diabetes and hypothyroidism, exercise level, and excessive weight are also known to influence cholesterol. The effects of heredity and disease cannot easily be changed. But doctors can help people control their cholesterol level by recommending increased exercise, weight loss, and, above all, dietary change. Exercise and weight loss have both been shown to help elevate the level of "good" (HDL) cholesterol in the bloodstream.

HEALTHY CHOICES

SATURATED FAT AND CHOLESTEROL CONTENTS OF FOODS

Food	Saturated fat (g)	Cholesterol (mg)
Cheddar cheese (1 oz)	6.0	30
Mozzarella, part skim (1 oz)	3.1	15
Whole milk (1 cup)	5.1	33
Skim milk (1 cup)	0.3	4
Butter (1 tbsp)	7.1	31
Mayonnaise (1 tbsp)	1.7	8
Tuna in oil (3 oz)	1.4	55
Tuna in water (3 oz)	0.3	48
Lean ground beef, broiled (3 oz)	6.2	74
Leg of lamb, roasted (3 oz)	5.6	78
Bacon (3 slices)	3.3	16
Chicken breast, roasted (3 oz)	0.9	73

Source: U.S. Department of Agriculture.

HEALTHY CHOICES

By contrast, dietary change works by reducing LDL cholesterol. The most effective single step is to cut back on intake of saturated fats. Cholesterol-rich foods should also be avoided, though the evidence is that saturated fats are the greater contributor to blood cholesterol. (See chart: Saturated Fat and Cholesterol Contents of Foods.)

HEALTHY CHOICES

The National Cholesterol Education Program suggests that fats should account for no more than 30 percent of the calories consumed and that daily cholesterol intake should not exceed 300 milligrams. Saturated fat consumption can be reduced by using margarine made from corn, safflower, or sunflower oil instead of butter. Eating foods low in saturated fat and cholesterol such as fish, poultry, and skim or low-fat milk can also reduce cholesterol levels. A rule of thumb used to evaluate saturated fat content is: If it flies, swims, or grows in the ground, it is lower in saturated fat. (See also FAST FOOD; FOOD LABELING; BODY FAT; MEATS, EGGS, AND LEGUMES GROUP; RISK FACTORS; OBESITY.)

CROSS TRAINING

Cross training is working out regularly at more than one athletic activity. This method of training has several advantages. It provides good overall conditioning by exercising more muscle groups, reduces the chance of injury, and helps alleviate the boredom that can occur with a single-exercise program. RUNNING and SWIMMING are examples of well-matched cross-training activities. Running builds lower-body STRENGTH and *muscular endurance*, while swimming conditions the upper body. Both activities help develop cardiovascular ENDURANCE.

HEALTHY CHOICES

When planning a cross-training schedule, choose activities that work different parts of the body. Continually working at one activity can

Triathlons. *Triathlons—swimming 2 miles, cycling 100 miles, and running a marathon—are cross-training competitions that include some of the most physically fit athletes in the world.*

put too much stress on the same muscles and joints, increasing the risk of injury. By alternating rowing with CYCLING every other day, for instance, the different muscle groups get a rest between workouts. Also, if an injury occurs, it may be possible to continue to maintain fitness by engaging in the alternate activity. (See also AEROBIC EXERCISE; EXERCISE; FITNESS; FITNESS TRAINING; SPORTS AND FITNESS; WEIGHT TRAINING.)

▶ CYCLING

Cycling. *Cycling can be a very pleasant way to strengthen the heart and lungs and exercise leg muscles.*

Cycling, or bicycle riding, is an excellent form of AEROBIC EXERCISE. It strengthens the heart and lungs, builds leg muscles, and burns more than 400 calories per hour. Nearly anyone in good health can ride a bicycle. However, cycling requires more expensive equipment than some other aerobic activities, and it is not suitable for all weather conditions. Many fitness cyclists use indoor stationary bikes to avoid bad weather and road hazards.

Preparing to Ride Cycling includes casual riding, racing, and mountain biking (riding over rough, hilly terrains), as well as riding for fitness. For fitness cycling, choose a bike that has 10 to 12 speeds. A good quality bicycle can cost several hundred dollars, so make sure the one you choose fits your needs.

When you begin a cycling program, ride on paved roads over flat or gently rolling terrain. Start out riding for 30 to 45 minutes (less if you are very unfit) three times a week and work up to an hour or more. Pedal in a gear that allows a pace of about 60 to 80 pedal revolutions per minute. Pedaling too fast or too hard can lead to muscle soreness. Pedaling in a very high gear can also cause "biker's knee," a pain around the kneecap. (See also SPORTS INJURIES.)

Cycling Safety Safety is an important concern for cyclists. More than 1,000 Americans are killed each year in cycling accidents, and 85 percent

HEALTHY CHOICES
●●●●●●●●●●●●

of these die from head injuries. While riding, always wear a safety helmet approved by the American National Standards Institute (ANSI). Wear brightly colored clothing, keep an eye on traffic, and always use hand signals. Be alert to hazardous road conditions such as potholes, ice, storm drains, and railroad tracks. (See also FITNESS; FITNESS TRAINING; HEART RATE.)

▷ DAIRY PRODUCTS   see MILK AND MILK PRODUCTS GROUP

▷ DEHYDRATION

Dehydration is a condition in which the body's water level is dangerously low. WATER is essential for good health and accounts for about 55 to 70 percent of an adult's weight. A reduction of even 2 percent of the body's water can reduce the ability of cells and tissues to function properly.

Causes and Symptoms   Dehydration can be caused by excessive PERSPIRATION during exercise. The amount of water lost through perspiration is likely to be higher in hot or humid weather. Large amounts of water can also be lost when a person experiences persistent *vomiting* or *diarrhea*.

RISK FACTORS
▶ ▶ ▶ ▶ ▶ ▶

Symptoms of dehydration include severe thirst, dry lips and tongue, increased heart rate and breathing rate, low blood pressure, dizziness, nausea, and confusion. A frequent complication of dehydration is the loss of salt and other vital substances in the body, causing lethargy, headache, cramps, and pallor.

Prevention   The sense of thirst normally indicates when the water level in the body is low. When water loss is rapid, however, the normal thirst

Fluid Replacement Prevents Dehydration. *Adequate fluid intake during exercise is very important. Without enough fluids, the body can become dehydrated, which results in fatigue and reduced athletic abilities.*

mechanism may not keep up with water loss and may fail to warn of dehydration. Therefore, the best way to prevent dehydration is to drink water before, during, and after exercise, especially in hot weather. In addition, check your weight before and after a workout. A sensible guideline is to drink a pint (about 0.5 L) of water for each pound (about 0.5 kg) lost during exercise. Sports beverages are no better than water at preventing or treating dehydration. (See also BEVERAGES; SPORTS AND HEAT PROBLEMS.)

▶ DIET AIDS

Diet aids—including prescription and over-the-counter pills, powders, supplements, and surgical procedures—are tried by a large number of overweight people in search of a fast and easy way to lose weight. Some are effective to a certain degree and some are not, but most have drawbacks that must be carefully weighed against the possible benefits. In some cases the drawbacks of diet aids are serious enough to justify their use only by very obese people. For any diet aid to work, it must be part of a weight-loss plan that includes a reduced CALORIE intake and EXERCISE.

Among the drugs used for weight loss are over-the-counter *diet pills*. These are intended to act as *appetite suppressants* by blocking the desire to eat. Appetite suppressants containing the decongestant phenylpropanolamine have been found to be a safe and somewhat effective diet aid by the Food and Drug Administration. Recent studies, however, show that this drug may cause a dangerous rise in blood pressure.

Appetite suppressants containing the synthetic drug *amphetamine* are best used under medical supervision with extreme caution. Amphetamine (also called speed) is a strongly addictive *stimulant* that can have unpleasant side effects, such as sleeplessness, irritability, and depression. In addition, without changes in LIFESTYLE, most people gain back the weight they lose using amphetamines.

Diuretics and laxatives are sometimes used as diet aids, but they are not an effective way to lose weight in the form of excess fat. Instead, these drugs promote the loss of water weight and can lead to DEHYDRATION. Both can be harmful if taken for any length of time. The thyroid hormone *thyroxine* is sometimes prescribed by physicians to help people who are overweight because the thyroid gland is not active enough. Very few people, however, are overweight due to poor thyroid function.

Other diet aids include vitamin-enriched candies (sold as appetite suppressants), products high in FIBER (intended to make the stomach feel full), and various powders that are mixed with milk and consumed in place of meals.

Several manufacturers produce lines of DIET FOODS that can help reduce weight by providing controlled portions of low-calorie foods. These types of foods are expensive, however. Equivalent or superior low-calorie meals are easy to make at home.

Surgical procedures to help people lose weight include LIPOSUCTION (suctioning fat deposits from under the skin), wiring the jaw closed, stapling the stomach to make it smaller, bypassing part of the intestine to limit the process of DIGESTION, and inserting a balloon in the stomach to

Appetite Suppressants. *Some appetite suppressants contain the stimulant amphetamine. These diet aids are risky and should be used with great caution.*

make it feel full. These surgical procedures all involve some risk and can produce complications. They are meant to be undertaken as a last resort by extremely overweight people.

Carefully investigate any diet aid before trying it. Many are ineffective and a waste of money, and some are dangerous. There is no magic pill or quick-fix procedure that can substitute for eating a well-balanced, low-calorie diet and engaging in regular exercise. (See also APPETITE; DIETARY GUIDELINES; DIETS; FAD DIETS; NUTRITION; OBESITY; WEIGHT-LOSS STRATEGY; WEIGHT MANAGEMENT; DIURETIC, 7; LAXATIVES, 7.)

HEALTHY CHOICES

▶ DIETARY GUIDELINES

Dietary guidelines are recommendations designed to encourage healthy eating habits. Guidelines are issued by government or scientific agencies to promote proper NUTRITION and to reduce the occurrence of disease. They can also help people control their weight.

Dietary guidelines cover both the types and quantities of food that should be eaten daily (see graph: Comparison of Average American Diet and Recommended Diet). Often, they suggest how each day's calories should be distributed among the categories of NUTRIENTS: FATS, PROTEINS, CARBOHYDRATES, VITAMINS, and MINERALS. They may recommend limiting the consumption of foods, such as fats, SALT, and SUGAR, that are known to contribute to certain diseases. They may also recommend eating more of certain foods that are essential to maintaining good health, such as those high in FIBER.

The nature of dietary guidelines has changed over the years. In the 1940s government authorities were concerned primarily about inadequate

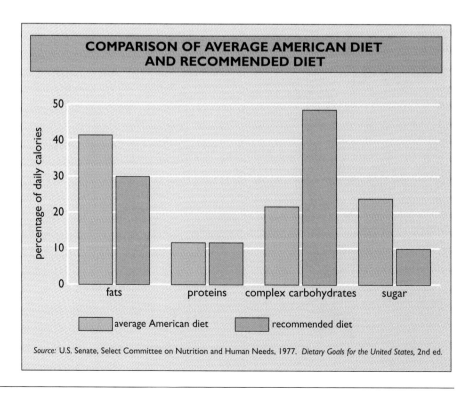

COMPARISON OF AVERAGE AMERICAN DIET AND RECOMMENDED DIET

percentage of daily calories

fats · proteins · complex carbohydrates · sugar

☐ average American diet   ☐ recommended diet

Source: U.S. Senate, Select Committee on Nutrition and Human Needs, 1977. *Dietary Goals for the United States*, 2nd ed.

nutrition in the population. Today, they are also concerned about excess consumption of certain foods. Guidelines issued by different organizations may vary depending upon the health concerns they address.

The *Dietary Guidelines for Americans*, produced by the U.S. Department of Agriculture and the U.S. Department of Health and Human Services, encourage people to eat a balanced diet and to limit the consumption of less nutritious foods. The official guidelines as of 1990 are summarized as follows:

HEALTHY CHOICES

▶ Eat a variety of foods.
▶ Maintain healthy weight.
▶ Choose a diet low in fat, saturated fat, and cholesterol.
▶ Choose a diet that includes plenty of vegetables, fruits, and grain products.
▶ Use sugars only in moderation.
▶ Use salt and sodium only in moderation.
▶ If you drink alcoholic beverages, do so in moderation.

(See also CALORIE; CHOLESTEROL; FOOD GROUP SYSTEMS; RECOMMENDED DIETARY ALLOWANCE; WEIGHT MANAGEMENT.)

▶ DIET FOOD

Diet food is primarily intended for weight loss. Many food manufacturers produce specially prepared diet foods that have closely controlled portions and/or reduced CALORIES and FATS. Some of these foods are healthful for other reasons as well. For example, low-sodium dishes help control blood pressure.

Reading labels is important to making informed choices about the variety of diet foods on the market, and manufacturers' terminology can be tricky. By law, any food that is labeled "low calorie" must have fewer than 40 calories per serving. A food labeled "reduced calorie" must have one-third fewer calories than does the food to which it is being compared. Until recently, the term *light* (or *lite*) had no standard definition. It has been used to make claims about calorie or fat content that can be misleading. For example, a label boasting that a "light" product is "94 percent fat-free" misleads the consumer because such a product is quite high in fat. Generally, a product with 3 grams of fat per serving is low in fat, 4 to 6 grams is a moderate fat content, and 7 grams or more is high in fat. However, in 1992 the Food and Drug Administration announced that it was introducing standard definitions of terms such as *light* and *low-fat*.

Prepared diet foods come in many different forms. A variety of diet frozen entrees are available. Diet foods such as soda, candy, and yogurt are often made with an ARTIFICIAL SWEETENER. Diet snack foods are those that have been baked (not fried) to reduce the amount of fats. A variety of diet desserts are on the market, including those using skim in place of whole milk or those using *fat substitutes* such as Simplesse.

Diet foods should only be used as part of a WEIGHT-LOSS STRATEGY that includes a well-balanced diet and regular EXERCISE. FAD DIETS, popular diets that do not provide complete NUTRITION, can be dangerous. And although these foods can be effective, foods that are naturally low in

Diet Meals. *A variety of foods are now available to meet the needs of people on weight-loss diets.*

calories are also easily prepared at home and probably cost less. (See also APPETITE; DIET AIDS; DIETARY GUIDELINES; DIETS; FOOD LABELING; OBESITY; WEIGHT MANAGEMENT.)

► DIETS

A diet is the types of foods an individual eats on a regular basis. A healthy and balanced diet is essential to maintain good health, repair damaged body tissues, and satisfy the body's energy needs. Some people require modified diets to fulfill special needs: Children and pregnant women require diets that promote growth, and people use diets to gain or lose weight, prevent or control illness, and boost athletic performance.

Elements of a Healthy Diet   A diet supplies CALORIES, which provide fuel for energy. The number of calories a person needs every day depends on age, size, fitness level, and lifestyle. The average adult man needs 2,500 calories a day; women generally need fewer. These requirements vary widely, however, depending on the level of physical activity of the individual. A diet should also supply a full range of NUTRIENTS: proteins, fats, carbohydrates, vitamins, and minerals. A variety of foods should be consumed to get the essential nutrients, including lean meats, poultry, and fish; low-fat dairy products; whole-grain breads and cereals; and fruits and vegetables. Nutritionists believe that for a *well-balanced diet*, 55 to 65 percent of your calories should come from foods high in CARBOHYDRATES, 25 to 30 percent should come from FATS, and 12 to 15 percent from PROTEINS.

Diets to Lose Weight   Losing excess weight will improve physical function and reduce the risk of a variety of diseases. An effective WEIGHT-LOSS STRATEGY reduces the number of calories but retains the same balance of nutrients necessary for good health. When dieting, make sure that daily VITAMIN and MINERAL requirements suggested in the RECOMMENDED DIETARY ALLOWANCES are met and that FIBER intake is maintained.

Losing weight is less difficult if you choose a diet that satisfies nutritional needs and does not cause excessive HUNGER and FATIGUE. Losing weight is also made easier and more effective by combining a diet with regular EXERCISE. Regular exercise plus a healthier diet should be made permanent in order to keep the weight off.

Resist extreme measures to lose weight, and beware of programs that promise quick and easy weight loss. They are often expensive and ineffective; some are dangerous. Many FAD DIETS cause a loss of muscle tissue and fluids that can lead to serious illness. (See also DIET FOOD.)

Diets to Gain Weight   Increasing the amount of fats in the diet is a fast way to gain weight, but a high-fat diet is unhealthy and results in increased body fat instead of lean tissue. To promote gains of muscle tissue, increase intake of nutritious foods, eat more frequently, and exercise vigorously. (See also WEIGHT-GAIN STRATEGY.)

Vegetarian Diets   A VEGETARIAN DIET excludes animal products like meat. *Vegans*, or *strict vegetarians*, also exclude eggs and dairy products and may need vitamin supplements. Vegetarians rely on alternative

Fad Diets. *Some weight-loss programs are based on diets that are not well balanced. Nutritionists now believe that the relative proportions of the various nutrients should be the same for a basic healthy diet and a diet to lose or gain weight.*

sources for protein, such as beans, nuts, eggs, and cheese. A move in the direction of vegetarian eating is increasingly seen as a healthy trend.

Diets for Athletes An athlete who actively trains and competes may have extraordinarily high energy needs. Daily calorie requirements for long-distance runners, for example, may be as high as 6,000 to 10,000 calories. Extra energy expenditure increases the need for VITAMIN B COMPLEX, so a high-performance diet should include *complex carbohydrates* and low-fat foods. Suggested foods include breads, cereals, fruits, and vegetables. Plenty of fluids should also be consumed before, during, and after exercise.

Diets to Treat and Prevent Illness Patients recovering from various disorders or people with normal health but special nutritional requirements may have special diets. For example, a *bland diet,* a diet that is easy to digest, may be prescribed for someone who is recovering from an illness or has a gastrointestinal disorder. A *high-calcium diet* is often prescribed for pregnant and nursing women. Extra calcium intake is also recommended for women to help prevent the bone-damaging condition called osteoporosis. Calcium-rich foods include milk, cheese, fish, broccoli, and spinach. A *low-fat diet* (especially one low in saturated fat) is one of the most effective ways of lowering blood CHOLESTEROL, so it is often prescribed for patients at risk for atherosclerosis and coronary artery disease. High-fat foods (whole-milk products, butter, cheese, pastry, nuts, peanut butter, creamy sauces) are limited to make up no more than 30 percent of calories consumed, and saturated fat should be no more than 7 to 10 percent of total calories. A low-fat diet is also advised for patients with gallbladder disease and is believed to reduce the chances of various forms of cancer. A *low-sodium diet* helps people who have a tendency to retain body fluids as a result of kidney or liver disease, high blood pressure, or congestive heart failure. Salty foods (bacon, ham, sausage, ice cream, chocolates, cheese, canned meat and fish, cakes and cookies, and salted condiments) are excluded from this diet. A *low-fiber* *diet* is recommended for people who have certain digestive disorders. Easily digested foods (eggs, milk, creamed soup, and cooked vegetables) are eaten in small amounts at frequent intervals. A *high-fiber diet* will help relieve constipation. It consists of foods such as whole-grain bread and cereals and raw and stewed fruit and vegetables. A *low-purine diet*— foods low in fat and high in carbohydrates—is advised for people who have gout. Recommended foods include skim milk, fruit, vegetables, and enriched bread and cereals. A *gluten-free diet* helps patients with celiac disease or nontropical sprue. These conditions result from sensitivity to the protein gluten, which is found in wheat, barley, and rye. Any foods containing these cereals must be eliminated from the diet. A *diabetic diet*, important for controlling diabetes mellitus, contains little sugar and includes carefully balanced amounts of calories, carbohydrates, protein, and fat. A varied diet is possible by following a system of food exchanges developed by the American Diabetes Association. (See also APPETITE; DIETARY GUIDELINES; FIBER; FOOD GROUP SYSTEMS; NUTRITION; PHYTOCHEMICALS; WEIGHT MANAGEMENT.)

► DIGESTION

Digestion is the process of breaking down food into simpler substances for use by the body. The end products of digestion are absorbed through the intestinal wall and into the bloodstream and distributed to all the cells of the body for nourishment.

All foods contain NUTRIENTS, which are divided into five groups: vitamins, minerals, carbohydrates, proteins, and fats. Most nutrients in food must be broken down by digestion into simpler elements before they can be used (VITAMINS and MINERALS, however, are absorbed into the bloodstream without change). For example, certain CARBOHYDRATES (starches and complex sugars) are broken down into simpler sugars, which the body uses for energy. PROTEINS are converted to substances that the body uses to repair and replace cells. FATS are changed during digestion to substances that help provide energy and store vitamins.

> Most nutrients in food must be broken down by digestion into simpler elements before they can be used.

How Digestion Works   The *digestive system* uses a series of physical and chemical processes. These processes begin in the mouth, where food is ground into smaller pieces and mixed with saliva. Saliva contains a digestive juice that begins to reduce carbohydrates to simpler sugars. After the food is swallowed, it moves through the esophagus by a series of muscular contractions to the stomach. Food is broken into smaller particles by the stomach's churning action. Acids and digestive juices chemically simplify the nutrients. In the small intestine, fluids (bile) produced by the liver and stored in the gallbladder separate fats into smaller particles. Secretions from the pancreas further break down carbohydrates, fats, and proteins. Enzymes produced by the small intestine complete the changes that food undergoes in the digestive system. The final products of this process are absorbed through the lining of the small intestine into the bloodstream or lymphatic system. Finally, undigestible matter such as FIBER passes into the large intestine and is expelled as feces.

Digestive Problems   Digestion can be disrupted by any problem that affects the breakdown and absorption of nutrients or prevents food from traveling through the digestive system. Examples include congenital abnormalities, infections, vomiting, heartburn, ulcers, inflammatory and autoimmune disorders, tumors, and allergic conditions.

HEALTHY CHOICES
▪●●●●●●●●●●●▪

Maintaining Good Digestion   A healthy, well-balanced diet with plenty of fiber helps maintain healthy digestion. Additional LIFESTYLE factors that contribute to good digestion include adequate sleep, regular exercise, and setting aside a relaxed period for mealtimes. (See also APPETITE; BODY METABOLISM; ENERGY, FOOD; HUNGER; DIGESTIVE SYSTEM, 1.)

▶ ## EATING DISORDERS

Eating disorders are health problems characterized by extremely harmful eating patterns. The two common eating disorders are anorexia (sometimes called anorexia nervosa) and bulimia. They are different problems but may arise from the same causes. Sometimes the two conditions are found together, or one may lead to the other.

Both anorexia and bulimia are most common in adolescent girls and young women. Only a small percentage of those with these disorders are male. Both conditions can have damaging effects on the body and even cause death. Medical and psychological treatment are usually needed to overcome the abnormal eating patterns.

Symptoms of Anorexia   People with anorexia starve themselves because they have an irrational fear of becoming fat. At the beginning, people with anorexia may merely go on a diet. Soon the idea of losing weight—as well as food itself—becomes an obsession. In addition to dieting, people with anorexia may exercise constantly to lose more and more weight. Even when they become extremely thin, they see themselves as fat (see illustration: Distorted Body Image). As a great deal of weight is lost, they feel the physical effects of MALNUTRITION, including FATIGUE. Women with anorexia often stop menstruating and may grow fine body hair called *lanugo*. Self-starvation often leads to heart and kidney disorders. Psychological problems, including depression, usually appear as well. Unless medical help is provided, body weight can drop to a dangerously low level.

Causes and Treatment of Anorexia   Anorexia is probably caused by a combination of factors. The tendency to develop it may be inherited, but psychological pressure seems to bring out the condition. People who have anorexia are often high achievers. They typically try hard to please the people around them and have low self-esteem. They may also have an unusually strong fear of growing up.

Experts believe that anorexia has a social basis as well. The frequency of the disease has increased greatly in the last 25 to 30 years, an era that has increasingly seen notions of beauty strongly linked with thinness. As a result, some people may become unhappy and feel unattractive when they are not "thin enough." The pressure to be thin is particularly strong for young women.

Distorted Body Image. *People with anorexia perceive themselves as "too fat," no matter how thin they really are. They see a distorted image of themselves and starve themselves to change it.*

Treatment of anorexia combines medical care with psychological counseling. Convincing people with the condition that they have a problem and need help can be difficult. Feeding to regain the lost weight and diet and psychological counseling to break harmful eating patterns are both important. Long-term care is usually needed to prevent the problem from returning.

Symptoms of Bulimia   Bulimia is a disorder that involves eating binges followed by self-induced vomiting. The binge eating and vomiting can lead to serious physical problems. Like anorexia, bulimia is related to a fear of gaining weight. However, it differs from anorexia in certain ways. People with bulimia do not necessarily lose as much weight as do those with anorexia. In addition, people with bulimia usually realize they have a problem that they cannot control.

Bulimia often begins with an attempt to diet. When people with bulimia become hungry, they have an eating binge. They typically consume (usually in secret) large quantities of high-calorie foods in a short time. Then they cause themselves to vomit, or use laxatives, in order to get rid of the food and prevent a weight gain. This soon becomes a pattern. Over time, binge eating can cause the stomach to enlarge. Vomiting can cause rashes, swollen ankles and feet, dehydration, rupture of the stomach or esophagus, and tooth damage because of excessive contact with stomach acid.

RISK FACTORS
▶ ▶ ▶ ▶ ▶ ▶

Causes and Treatment of Bulimia   Bulimia is often caused by the same factors that lead to anorexia. People with bulimia tend to set very high standards for themselves, but they have low self-esteem. They are troubled by the same social pressures to be thin that cause anorexia and have similar preoccupation with food and eating.

Treatment for people with bulimia is similar to treatment for those with anorexia. They need a combination of medical care and psychological counseling to break out of the binge eating and vomiting cycle. They often need ongoing support in order to stay well.

CONSULT A
PHYSICIAN

Confronting Eating Disorders   Today there are many sources of help for people with eating disorders. Treatment centers and teams of medical professionals specialize in these conditions. If you think you may have an eating disorder, or suspect one in someone you know, get medical help as early as possible. It may take several attempts to get a person with anorexia to accept help, but it is important to keep trying. Treatment programs can break harmful eating patterns and replace them with healthful eating habits. Counseling can also provide continuing support to prevent the problem from recurring. (See also FASTING; FOOD CRAVING; UNDERWEIGHT; WEIGHT ASSESSMENT; ANOREXIA/BULIMIA, 5.)

▶ **ENDURANCE**   Endurance, or stamina, is the body's ability to perform a prolonged physical activity without tiring. Endurance, STRENGTH, and FLEXIBILITY are the basic elements of physical FITNESS.

Endurance is made up of two components—*cardiovascular endurance* and *muscular endurance*. A strong heart pumps greater amounts of oxygen-rich blood, while strong muscles extract and use oxygen efficiently. The endurance of both the heart and muscles can be increased by regular prolonged EXERCISE.

Increasing Cardiovascular Endurance   The cardiovascular system—the heart, lungs, and blood vessels—delivers oxygen throughout the body, including the muscles. Cardiovascular fitness is increased through regular AEROBIC EXERCISE, such as walking, swimming, running, cycling, rowing, sports requiring a lot of running, and cross-country skiing. This kind of exercise requires the cardiovascular system to work harder to meet the body's higher oxygen needs. During intense aerobic exercise, the heart rate can rise as much as 400 percent, increasing the amount of blood pumped from 5 quarts (4.7 L) a minute to as many as 20 quarts (19 L) a minute. Regular aerobic exercise builds the heart's endurance by strengthening and thickening the walls of its pumping chamber, which increases the amount of blood pumped with each heartbeat.

Increasing Muscular Endurance   Training increases the number of capillaries in the muscles, so the muscles can receive more blood during exercise. In addition, the activity of certain chemicals in the muscles called *enzymes* increases with exercise, allowing muscles to extract and use oxygen more efficiently. This improves muscular endurance.

There are several ways to increase muscular endurance. Regular aerobic exercise (three or four times a week) will help achieve muscular endurance for the specific muscles exercised. Running, for example, can greatly improve endurance in the legs but will do little to build endurance in the upper body. Endurance training requires regular workouts that place heavy, repeated demands on muscle groups for progressively longer periods of time. It differs from strength training, which emphasizes the amount of resistance placed against the muscles. Endurance training tends to use less resistance for more repetitions of a given exercise. A recommended training schedule is three times a week, with at least a day of rest between workouts to prevent muscle fatigue, soreness, and injury. (See also STRENGTH EXERCISE; WEIGHT TRAINING.)

Building Endurance. *Increasing cardiovascular endurance is probably the most important aspect of overall fitness.*

HEALTHY CHOICES

▶ **ENERGY, FOOD**   Food energy is the fuel that the human body needs to function. People need energy for every process of living: to breathe, to move, to think, to grow, and to maintain body temperature, for example. They get their energy from NUTRIENTS in the food they eat.

How Food Becomes Energy   When a person eats food, the nutrients in CARBOHYDRATES, FATS, and PROTEINS are converted into fuel for the body. GLUCOSE, a type of SUGAR and the body's primary fuel, is used to produce energy as soon as it enters the bloodstream. *Metabolism* is the process of changing food into energy or into substances the body can use. (See also BODY METABOLISM.)

Not all the energy value of food is used immediately. Some is stored for later use. Some glucose is stored in the liver and muscles in the form of *glycogen*. Energy is also stored in the form of fat, some under the skin

Food Energy. *Starch is a carbohydrate found in grains and vegetables, and it is the primary energy source for people.*

and some around vital organs. The *fatty acids,* which are combined with glycerol to form fat, are the body's long-term energy reserve and are available for conversion to energy as needed. (See also LIVER, **1**.)

Measuring Food Energy   The energy potential of food is measured by a unit of heat called a CALORIE. A food's calorie count is the amount of energy the food provides when metabolized. When energy—either from body fat or from food—is used by the body, the process is called burning calories.

In the long term, a person's weight stability depends on the balance between energy intake (calories consumed) and energy output (calories burned). When intake is greater, weight is gained; when output is greater, weight is lost; and when they are equal, weight is stable. (See also ENERGY, PHYSICAL; WEIGHT MANAGEMENT.)

ENERGY, PHYSICAL   Physical energy is the body's capacity for doing work. People need physical energy for every action, from running a marathon to keeping their heart beating. They also need energy to allow their muscles to recover.

How the Body Produces Energy   Bodily energy comes from NUTRIENTS in the food we eat and oxygen in the air we breathe. These are converted by the body into the many different chemicals that make up all our cells and body fluids—including the major substances that supply energy: GLUCOSE and BODY FAT. (See also ENERGY, FOOD.)

To generate energy for movement, the body actually relies on instant chemical change within the muscle cells themselves—no substances from

CALORIES BURNED IN VARIOUS ACTIVITIES

Activity	Per pound every 10 min	By a 120-lb person every 10 min	By a 190-lb person every 10 min
Bicycling Moderate (10 mph)	0.5	60	95
Football (touch)	0.40	48	76
Handball	0.63	76	120
Hiking	0.42	50	80
Judo and karate	0.87	104	165
Running 10 mph (6 min/mi)	1	120	190
Skiing (snow) Downhill	0.59	71	112
Cross-country	0.78	94	148
Soccer	0.63	76	120
Swimming (crawl) 20 yd/min	0.32	38	61
Tennis Moderate	0.46	55	87
Volleyball	0.36	43	68
Walking 2 mph	0.22	26	42
Basal metabolism Man	0.076	9.1	14
Woman	0.068	8.2	13

Source: Levy, Marvin R., Mark Dignan, and Janet H. Shirreffs. 1992. *Life & health: Targeting wellness.* New York: McGraw-Hill.

> The energy output of the body is measured in calories—the same units that are used to measure the energy contained in food.

outside are needed. But after the muscle has contracted a few times, the chemicals in the cells must be restored to their former state. This is when the energy substances are used or *burned*, in a relatively slow chemical reaction during which they are broken down and combined with oxygen. Thus, working muscles need a steady supply not only of oxygen from the blood but also of energy substances from the digestion of food. These substances come chiefly from the CARBOHYDRATES and FATS that we eat, though PROTEINS can also be used for energy.

The energy output of the body is measured in CALORIES—the same units that are used to measure the energy contained in foods. This enables nutritionists to monitor the relationship between diet, exercise, and weight gain or loss.

Calorie Requirements for Energy   Calorie requirements differ depending on the *basal metabolic rate* and the level of physical activity. Basal metabolic rate is the speed at which the body burns calories to handle its basic processes, when it is neither digesting nor involved in exercise. It differs from person to person and is affected by many factors, including body weight. The amount of calories burned in exercise is also affected by weight (see chart: Calories Burned in Various Activities). (See also BODY METABOLISM.)

Muscular activities and basal metabolism affect the number of calories a person needs every day. But you do not need highly detailed knowledge of your metabolism to figure out your own energy needs. Monitor your food intake and body weight during several weeks of typical activity. If your weight remains the same, your energy needs are balanced. (See also EXERCISE; REST; WEIGHT MANAGEMENT.)

► EXCHANGE SYSTEM

The exchange system is a method of diet planning that groups foods according to CALORIES and the amount of NUTRIENTS such as PROTEINS, CARBOHYDRATES, and FATS they contain. Foods within each group can be exchanged for each other. The system is useful for people who need to keep track of the number of calories in their food while maintaining a balanced diet.

How the System Works   Foods are divided into six groups in the exchange system. The groups are:

- ► Milk
- ► Vegetables
- ► Fruit
- ► Starch and bread
- ► Meat and meat alternatives
- ► Fat

> Each unit of food in the group is called an exchange. One small apple is one fruit exchange. The apple can be exchanged for half of a small banana.

Each group has a standard food with a specified portion size. For the milk group, for example, it is 1 cup (237 mL) of nonfat milk. The other foods in the group have similar amounts of carbohydrate, protein, fat, and calories. Each unit of food in the group is called an exchange. One small apple is one fruit exchange. The apple can be exchanged for one half of a small banana; a whole banana is considered two fruit exchanges. Some of the exchanges are smaller than are servings in other diet systems. A meat exchange, for example, is 1 ounce (28 g). A 3-ounce (85-g) serving of meat would count as three meat exchanges.

There are some surprises in the way foods are grouped in the exchange system. Grouping foods according to carbohydrate, protein, and fat content brings together foods that would be in different groups in another system. For example, cheese is in the meat exchange group, because the carbohydrate, protein, and fat content of cheese is similar to that of meat. Bacon and olives are in the fat group because both have very high fat content. The groupings highlight useful nutritional similarities among foods.

Using the System   A diet based on the exchange system would specify the number of exchanges to be chosen daily from each group. For example, a diet of 2,000 calories per day might include: 10 bread exchanges, 6 meat exchanges, 4 vegetable exchanges, 5 fruit exchanges, 2 milk exchanges, and 7 fat exchanges. A variety of foods could be selected to meet the exchange totals for the day.

Planning a diet according to the exchange system is a complex process. First, you must determine how many calories should be consumed daily. Then you consult a table that tells how many food exchanges to consume from each group in order to obtain those calories. Last, you must consult exchange group lists to see which foods to eat in which quantities. Although complicated at first, the exchange system can be useful in regulating calories because it is precise. Most people find that the exchange allowances and groups become familiar when they are used regularly. (See also DIETARY GUIDELINES; FIVE FOOD GROUPS SYSTEM; FOOD GROUP SYSTEMS; FOOD PYRAMID SYSTEM; FOUR FOOD GROUPS SYSTEM.)

▶ **EXERCISE**

Exercise is physical activity for the purpose of recreation or FITNESS. It is generally thought of as being separate from the movements and exertions required by work and everyday life. For most Americans, whose work and everyday life tend to be relatively inactive, regular exercise is essential to overall health.

Health and Exercise Adequate levels of activity and movement are necessary to keep the human body fit. Regular exercise is what keeps its major components strong and in working order. Exercise also speeds BODY METABOLISM, increasing the rate at which CALORIES are burned.

HEALTHY CHOICES

Any amount of exercise is beneficial. But in order to obtain a significant health benefit, most experts recommend that exercise be regular (at least three times a week), last long enough (a minimum of 20 to 30 minutes a session), be strenuous enough, and work as many parts of the body as possible. People who exercise regularly are healthier than those who do not. As a group, they are sick less often and live longer. They experience fewer serious medical conditions and diseases, including heart disease, hypertension, osteoporosis, and even cancer. They have less difficulty managing their weight and therefore avoid the health problems associated with OBESITY.

Exercise has significant psychological benefits as well. It reduces stress and promotes relaxation. People who exercise also tend to have a greater sense of general well-being and higher levels of self-esteem than those who do not.

Forms of Exercise Any activity that requires a body to move and work can be a form of exercise; the possibilities are endless. One useful way to categorize forms of exercise, however, is by their purpose. Some types of exercise, including many sports, games, and outdoor activities, are intended primarily for recreation. Others, such as riding an exercise bicycle or running on a treadmill, are primarily intended to promote fitness. Many forms of exercise, however, serve both purposes.

Exercise can also be categorized by the demands it places on the heart and lungs. AEROBIC EXERCISE, such as distance running, demands

Exercise. *Because many people's daily routines involve little exercise, they need to plan a regular exercise program to stay fit.*

CONSULT A
PHYSICIAN

HEALTHY CHOICES

increased supplies of oxygen for extended periods of time. As a result, it increases the HEART RATE and the rate of breathing in order to supply extra oxygen to the body. Aerobic exercises are among the most desirable from a health standpoint, particularly for the cardiovascular system. ANAEROBIC EXERCISE is characterized by short bursts of intensive physical exertion, such as sprinting. These demanding activities require more oxygen than the cardiovascular system can rush to body tissues on a short-term basis, creating an *oxygen debt*. Anaerobic exercise can be sustained only for a brief time and has relatively little benefit for the heart and lungs.

Exercise Precautions   Exercise is not without risks, particularly of injury. Generally, the more strenuous and demanding the activity, the greater the chances of injury. By taking some basic precautions, however, you can greatly reduce the risks of exercising:

▸ Avoid the temptation to do too much too soon. This is especially important if you have not been exercising regularly.
▸ Begin each exercise session by gradually warming up your muscles and joints with STRETCHING EXERCISES.
▸ Avoid exercising in extremely hot or extremely cold weather.
▸ Drink plenty of water before, during, and after exercise sessions to reduce the chances of DEHYDRATION.
▸ Pay attention to your body. Stop exercising if you feel breathless, nauseated, or dizzy. If you feel acute pain in your chest or radiating through your shoulder or arm for more than 2 minutes, seek medical attention immediately.
▸ Do not eat meals or drink alcohol too soon before an exercise session.

Exercise and Lifestyle   An active person is a healthy person. By making exercise a regular and enjoyable part of your LIFESTYLE, you can significantly improve your health and well-being. The more habitual exercise becomes, the more likely you are to experience its many benefits. (See also ENERGY, PHYSICAL; EXERCISE MACHINES; FITNESS TRAINING; RISK FACTORS; SPORTS AND FITNESS; STRENGTH EXERCISE; WEIGHT MANAGEMENT.)

► **EXERCISE MACHINES**   Exercise machines provide a variety of methods to enhance fitness. Used at a gym or at home, each machine has its own particular advantages. Some, such as stationary bicycles and treadmills, provide an excellent way to get AEROBIC EXERCISE. Others, such as weight machines, are used primarily to build muscle STRENGTH. Used in combination, or properly coordinated with other forms of regular EXERCISE, these machines can be a valuable part of an overall FITNESS program. All of them offer the advantage of being able to be used indoors, regardless of the weather.

Stationary Bicycles   The most popular home exercise machine is the stationary bike. Bicycling in place on such a machine provides an excellent aerobic workout and builds leg strength and endurance by providing

Stationary Bike. *A stationary bike is a relatively affordable machine that can be used at home. It offers a variety of workout benefits, such as increased muscular endurance and strength as well as cardiovascular conditioning.*

resistance as you pedal. Machines that allow for the use of the arms while pedaling, such as the Schwinn AirDyne, help build upper-body strength as well. A good stationary bike has a sturdy frame, comfortable seat, smooth pedaling action, and simple controls for adjusting the level of resistance. Some models include ergometers—devices that measure the amount of work done, sometimes measured as calories burned. These are not necessary, however, because you can use your heart rate and a clock to measure the effectiveness of your workout and your progress from session to session.

Rowing Machines   By duplicating the action of rowing a boat, a rowing machine combines an aerobic workout with strength and endurance training for the major muscles of the back, arms, shoulders, and legs. Most rowing machines use adjustable hydraulic pistons to produce resistance. Look for a sturdy model that has a sliding seat, smooth action, and convenient, adjustable controls.

Cross-Country Ski Machines   Another popular type of exercise machine simulates cross-country skiing to provide exercise year-round. A ski machine develops aerobic conditioning, endurance in arm and leg muscles, and coordination and FLEXIBILITY. This device has short skis on rollers with cables or poles for the arms. Many models have adjustable resistance for both arms and legs. As with other exercise machines, sturdiness, smooth action, and easy-to-use controls are key features.

Treadmills and Stair-Climbers   Treadmills are machines that allow you to walk or run in place. The best kind of treadmill is motorized to

Exercise Equipment. *A spa or gym offers a variety of machines to plan a fitness program that best suits individual needs.*

drive the tread at varying speeds but has the disadvantage of being expensive and bulky. Treadmills offer a cardiovascular workout and endurance training for leg muscles. However, these benefits can be duplicated by jogging in place. Stair-climbing machines are a variation of a treadmill that simulates climbing steps, but again the benefit can also be achieved by climbing flights of stairs.

Weight Machines   Weight machines such as Nautilus, Cybex, and Universal, also called *resistance equipment,* can be used to exercise all the major muscle groups in the body to increase strength and flexibility. Although the use of this equipment should be learned with the help of an instructor, once learned, weight machines are safe and easy to use. Many of the benefits of weight machines are similar to the benefits of free weights. Free weights, however, have the added benefit of improving coordination and balance with the effort to lift and hold the weights overhead. Resistance training offers very little cardiovascular training, however, so regular aerobic exercise should be a part of a total FITNESS TRAINING routine. (See also CROSS TRAINING; ENDURANCE; WEIGHT TRAINING.)

▶ FAD DIETS

A fad diet is any weight-loss diet that is nutritionally unsound. Most fad diets promise quick results; often they produce considerable weight loss at the outset—much of it water. But generally they are ineffective because weight lost is usually gained back again. Some fad diets are dangerous and have caused serious illnesses and death. Fad diets include liquid diets, diets that provide very few calories, diets that are restricted to only one or two foods, and diets that severely restrict or eliminate a food group or major nutrient.

An example of a fad diet is the high-protein, low-carbohydrate diet that was popular for several years. This type of diet is not healthy. It tends to be high in fat and can result in high levels of blood CHOLESTEROL, abnormal heart rhythms, and excessive strain on the kidneys. In the 1970s, a high-protein liquid diet apparently caused 58 people to die suddenly from heart rhythm problems.

The formulas of liquid diets have been improved, but most are intended only for the very obese—people who are at least 30 percent OVERWEIGHT. These diets are to be administered only under the supervision of a doctor. The widely available diet powders that are used at home are safe as long as at least one well-balanced meal a day and plenty of water are also consumed. But these diets are largely ineffective, because most people gain the weight back.

Losing and gaining weight in cycles—the so-called *yo-yo syndrome*—is a problem for many people. In the yo-yo syndrome, weight loss is often rapid at first. The reduced caloric intake, however, causes the *metabolic rate* to slow down and food energy to be conserved by the body. Because the body is using food at a slower rate, weight loss through dieting becomes increasingly difficult. When the fad diet is abandoned, the slower metabolic rate results in a rapid increase in weight. Often, the person ends up weighing more than he or she weighed before the diet.

Over-the-Counter Liquid Diets.
The widely available liquid diets are especially likely to result in weight rebound because they do nothing to improve the eating habits and sedentary living that led to the excessive weight in the first place.

HEALTHY CHOICES
●●●●●●●●●●●●●

For an effective WEIGHT-LOSS STRATEGY, nutritionists and physicians recommend a well-balanced diet of no fewer than 1,200 calories a day. Weight loss should be slow and steady—1 to 2 pounds per week. A regular AEROBIC EXERCISE program will also help burn fat and increase metabolic rate. A lifelong change in habits is necessary to eliminate unhealthy and fattening eating practices. (See also DIET AIDS; DIETS; FASTING; MALNUTRITION; OBESITY; WEIGHT MANAGEMENT.)

▶ FAST FOOD

Fast food is mass-produced food that is served ready to eat at restaurants and food stands. Popular fast food includes hamburgers, french fries, pizza, doughnuts, fried chicken, hot dogs, and tacos. Most fast foods are high in CALORIES, FATS, SALT, and SUGAR, but low in other NUTRIENTS. For that reason, nutritionists recommend that you make fast foods only a small part of your diet.

Each day, about one-third of the foods Americans eat are fast foods. On the plus side, fast foods typically supply ample amounts of CARBOHYDRATES and PROTEINS. However, they are usually low in vitamins and minerals. And some fast foods are so high in calories, that they provide as much as half of an average person's daily calorie needs. Unfortunately, a large proportion of the calories in fast foods comes from fats. For example, fat can make up nearly 50 percent of the calories in fried chicken or fish as the result of cooking oils trapped in the breading. Hamburgers, cheeseburgers, and french fries—the staples of fast food—are also very high in fat. In addition, many fast food "shakes" are made with high-fat vegetable oils instead of milk. Even salads and cole slaw can be very high in fat because of the mayonnaise or heavy, oily dressings used on them.

Fast Food. *When eating fast food, choose one of the lighter menu items available at many major fast-food restaurants.*

Fast-food restaurants are popular because they provide fast, convenient food for less money than do traditional restaurants. If you eat at a fast-food restaurant, try to choose foods that are nutritious and low in calories, such as a plain salad, grilled chicken, a plain baked potato, a slice of cheese pizza, a roast beef sandwich, or a taco. (See also FATS, OILS, AND SWEETS GROUP; JUNK FOOD.)

HEALTHY CHOICES
●●●●●●●●●●●●●

▶ FASTING

Fasting is deliberately abstaining from food for a period of time. It is required before some medical tests and procedures, and it is part of some religious observances. It is not recommended as a way of losing weight and can be dangerous.

The effect of prolonged fasting on the body is the same as starvation. When there is no energy available from food, the body turns to its own tissues for fuel. Reserves of carbohydrates are used first, then fat and muscle tissue is broken down. The rate of BODY METABOLISM slows to conserve energy. The body's resistance to infection is lowered, and the heart may be damaged. The digestive process may slow or stop entirely, and the production of sex hormones shuts down.

RISK FACTORS
▶ ▶ ▶ ▶ ▶ ▶

As fasting continues, weight loss slows down. This is because of the decreased rate of metabolism and because the body begins to conserve salt, causing water to be retained in the tissues. Prolonged fasting has health hazards that disqualify it as a weight-control method. In general, a person should not fast for more than 2 days without medical supervision. (See also FAD DIETS; WEIGHT-LOSS STRATEGY.)

▶ **FAT**

see BODY FAT

▶ **FATIGUE**

Fatigue is a feeling of weariness or tiredness. Fatigue can be caused by a lack of sleep, inadequate diet, physical or mental exertion, or psychological factors. Fatigue can also be a symptom of many different kinds of illnesses.

Types of Fatigue Many types of fatigue have a physical basis. Your sleep habits, diet, work or study habits, and physical activities can contribute to fatigue. Most fatigue that has a physical basis is normal and healthy. It is usually a signal that you need REST.

Fatigue may also have a psychological basis. Conflicts, stress, or boredom can result in weariness.

Physical or mental illness may cause fatigue as well. Physical sickness ranging from the flu to serious diseases such as anemia or diabetes make people feel very tired. In addition, mental illness such as severe depression or anxiety can cause fatigue.

Fatigue. *A fit person will recover quickly from the fatigue of a vigorous workout.*

Symptoms of Fatigue   Physical symptoms of fatigue include body weariness, aching muscles, a loss of coordination, and difficulty in performing physical tasks. Fatigue can also affect mental function, making it difficult to concentrate or make decisions. Fatigue should not be chronic. If it is, a physician or psychiatrist should be consulted.

How to Overcome Fatigue   Ordinarily, fatigue is simply overcome by getting rest or sleep. A change in diet might also be required. Fatigue that has a psychological basis is more difficult to overcome. People who are fatigued need to try to determine its cause so appropriate steps can be taken to resolve it. Doing so often requires psychological counseling. If a person cannot pinpoint the cause of fatigue, implementing a new routine or a change in LIFESTYLE can help. (See also MALNUTRITION; SLEEP, **1**; ANEMIA, **3**; CHRONIC FATIGUE SYNDROME, **3**.)

HEALTHY CHOICES

▶ FATS

Fats are one of the three *macronutrients*—classes of dietary nutrients that the body needs in large amounts. Fats serve many functions: They provide the body with its most concentrated form of energy, they are an important part of cell membranes, and as body fat, they cushion kidneys and other internal organs against sudden shock and insulate the body against loss of body heat. In addition, fats transport vitamins A, D, E, and K throughout the body.

Fats are found in varying concentrations in a wide range of foods (see chart: Fat Content of Foods). Measured in CALORIES, fats generate an average of 9 calories per gram as compared with the 4 or 5 calories per gram found in carbohydrates and proteins. This is what makes fats the most "fattening" foods to eat.

Although fats can create problems nutritionally, they are just as essential in the right amounts as PROTEINS and CARBOHYDRATES, the other macronutrients. Fats provide the body's large, long-term energy reserve, whereas reserves of carbohydrate energy are limited and can soon be exhausted.

Saturated Fats   The structure of dietary fats is determined by the number of hydrogen atoms that are attached to the carbon atoms of the molecule. These differing types of fats have different effects on health. Saturated fats have the maximum number of hydrogen atoms attached to each molecule. Generally, saturated fats are solid at room temperature. The amount of saturated fat in the diet should be limited, because this type of fat contributes to high blood cholesterol levels. High levels of CHOLESTEROL in the blood increase the risk of blocked arteries and atherosclerosis, coronary artery disease, and stroke. Most of the saturated fats come from animal sources and include butter, milk fat, and the fat found in meats. Among plants, coconut and palm oils are also highly saturated.

RISK FACTORS
▶ ▶ ▶ ▶ ▶ ▶

Unsaturated Fats   Unsaturated fats have not linked up with all the hydrogen atoms they can carry. Depending on how many slots for hydrogen atoms remain open, they are called either monounsaturated or polyunsaturated fats. Unsaturated fats are usually liquid at room temperature.

FAT CONTENT OF FOODS

Food	Saturated fat (g)	Monounsaturated fat (g)	Polyunsaturated fat (g)
Cheddar cheese (1 oz)	6.0	2.7	0.3
Mozzarella, part skim (1 oz)	3.1	1.4	0.1
Whole milk (1 cup)	5.1	2.4	0.3
Skim milk (1 cup)	0.3	0.1	—
Butter (1 tbsp)	7.1	3.3	0.4
Mayonnaise (1 tbsp)	1.7	3.2	5.8
Tuna in oil (3 oz)	1.4	1.9	3.1
Tuna in water (3 oz)	0.3	0.2	0.3
Lean ground beef, broiled (3 oz)	6.2	6.9	0.6
Leg of lamb, roasted (3 oz)	5.6	4.9	0.8
Bacon (3 slices)	3.3	4.5	1.1
Chicken breast, roasted (3 oz)	0.9	1.1	0.7

Source: U.S. Department of Agriculture.

Polyunsaturated fats can help lower blood cholesterol levels, perhaps by helping the body to excrete cholesterol. Some of the largely monounsaturated fats are peanut, avocado, and olive oils. Examples of mainly polyunsaturated fats are corn, sesame, and safflower oils. In order to make the unsaturated fats in margarines and shortenings harder and more stable, manufacturers add hydrogen atoms by a process called *hydrogenation*. Unsaturated fats that are artificially saturated, however, pose the same nutritional problems as saturated fats.

Dietary Guidelines Most Americans consume too much fat. On average, about 40 percent of their daily calories come from fats. According to most nutrition experts, people should consume no more than 30 percent of all calories in the form of dietary fats. Of this 30 percent, it is recommended that no more than 10 percent come from saturated fats, no more than 10 percent from polyunsaturated fats, and the remainder from monounsaturated fats. You can control your fat intake by cutting down on red meats, switching to low-fat dairy products, and avoiding fried foods. (See also BODY FAT; FAST FOOD; FATS, OILS, AND SWEETS GROUP; ENERGY, FOOD; NUTRIENTS; OBESITY.)

HEALTHY CHOICES
●●●●●●●●●●●●

► **FATS, OILS, AND SWEETS GROUP** The fats, oils, and sweets food group is a class of foods that are filling and often high in CALORIES but low in valuable NUTRIENTS. Foods in this group include butter, margarine, cooking oil, mayonnaise, cookies, jam, potato chips, pretzels, and soft drinks. Foods in this group are often high in FATS and SUGAR.

Fats, Oils, and Sweets Group.
Eat only small amounts of these foods, and never substitute foods from this group for more nutritious foods.

HEALTHY CHOICES

Everyone needs some fats in their diet. Fats help keep the skin and hair healthy, transport certain VITAMINS, and produce energy. But the relatively few fats you need are easily obtained from other, more nutritious foods, especially those of the MILK AND MILK PRODUCTS GROUP and the MEATS, EGGS, AND LEGUMES GROUP. Many of the foods in the fats, oils, and sweets group are high in saturated fats and CHOLESTEROL. *Saturated fats* are found mostly in foods that come from animals, and cholesterol is found only in animal products. High levels of saturated fats and cholesterol in the diet cause heart disease and atherosclerosis. Some studies have found links between diets high in fat and the incidence of certain kinds of cancer, especially breast cancer and colorectal cancer. In addition, because fats, oils, and sweets are so high in calories, they often produce an undesired weight gain and can lead to OBESITY and its various related health problems.

No daily serving suggestion is given for foods in this group in the FOUR FOOD GROUPS SYSTEM, the FIVE FOOD GROUPS SYSTEM, or the FOOD PYRAMID SYSTEM. All the systems suggest eating them only in small amounts and never substituting them for foods that are more nutritious. (See also BREADS AND CEREALS GROUP; DIETARY GUIDELINES; EXCHANGE SYSTEM; FOOD GROUP SYSTEMS; FRUITS AND VEGETABLES GROUP; ATHEROSCLEROSIS, 3; BREAST CANCER, 3; COLORECTAL CANCER, 3; HEART DISEASE, 3.)

FIBER

Fiber, or roughage, is the undigestible part of foods of plant origin. Fiber is a type of NUTRIENT called a complex CARBOHYDRATE, but unlike other carbohydrates, it does not produce energy. It is an important dietary component, however, because it aids DIGESTION. Foods high in fiber include whole grains, apples, beans, peas, corn, potatoes, and broccoli.

Types of Fiber   There are two kinds of fiber, soluble and insoluble. *Soluble fiber* dissolves in water. Oat bran and gummy fibers found in fruits (such as pectin, agar, and mucilage) are soluble. *Insoluble fibers* (cellulose, hemicellulose, and lignin) make up the cell walls of plants.

Function and Value of Fiber   As fiber passes through the large intestine, it absorbs large amounts of water and binds with digestive waste products. This creates large, soft stools that move through the digestive tract faster and are easier to eliminate.

HEALTHY CHOICES

Some research has associated a high-fiber diet with a lower risk of developing colon cancer, diabetes, and some disorders of the colon such as diverticulitis, constipation, and hemorrhoids. A diet high in fiber can also help people lose weight by filling the stomach without adding calories.

Some studies have indicated that soluble fiber may lower CHOLESTEROL in the bloodstream and help prevent heart disease, but the effect is modest.

The U.S. Food and Drug Administration recommends that people eat 20 to 35 grams of fiber a day. But the average American's diet includes only 11 grams of fiber. You can increase fiber intake by eating a

FIBER CONTENT IN SELECTED FOODS	
Food	**Dietary fiber (g)**
Whole-wheat bread (1 slice)	1.5
Corn bran, uncooked (⅓ cup)	20.4
Apple (1 small)	2.8
Pear (1 large)	2.9
Broccoli, cooked (½ cup)	2.4
Carrots, cooked (½ cup)	2.0
Kidney beans, cooked (½ cup)	6.9
Pinto beans, cooked (½ cup)	5.9

HEALTHY CHOICES
■●●●●●●●●●●●●●

high-fiber bran cereal for breakfast and more fruits and vegetables of all kinds during the course of the day. Whole-grain breads in place of white bread as well as nuts and seeds such as sunflower seeds will also add fiber to the diet (see chart: Fiber Content in Selected Foods). (See also DIETARY GUIDELINES.)

▶ FITNESS

Fitness is the body's ability to meet the varied physical demands of life. A function of conditioning, fitness is a key element in overall health, one that promotes general well-being.

Becoming fit requires activity in the form of EXERCISE. This can be work, play, sports, athletic training, or any other form of physical activity. In the past, when work was more physical, the daily LIFESTYLES of people normally required much more activity than is normal today, assuring a higher level of fitness. In the United States today, fitness levels have consequently declined, creating a serious health problem.

HEALTHY CHOICES
■●●●●●●●●●●●●

Eating a good diet and getting the right kind and amount of exercise are essential to becoming fit. For those who eat too much or get too little exercise, this requires significant lifestyle changes.

Fitness can be broken down in any of several ways. One useful way to think of fitness is to view it as having three primary components: strength, endurance, and flexibility. An additional aspect of fitness is body composition, the proportion of fat to lean tissue in the body.

Strength STRENGTH most commonly refers to *muscle strength*. It is the amount of force that muscles can exert when they contract. Muscle strength is necessary for all movement, which is created by the contraction of specific muscle groups. Strong muscles allow the body to move more efficiently and do more work. They also help support and protect many of the systems of the body, such as the joints and internal organs. Muscle strength can be improved with STRENGTH EXERCISE, which builds muscles by systematically requiring them to do greater amounts of work.

A strong heart is also necessary to be fit. A strong heart beats more strongly and can pump more blood, which is an essential part of cardiovascular health.

Bone strength is also important. Although more difficult to measure than muscle strength, bone strength is primarily determined by the density of bone mass. This can be improved with exercises that are weight-bearing, such as running and WEIGHT TRAINING.

Endurance ENDURANCE is the body's ability to sustain an activity or continue to perform work. *Muscular endurance* and *cardiovascular endurance* are the main components. Both are improved through regular AEROBIC EXERCISE, which requires the skeletal muscles, heart, vascular system, and lungs to work hard for prolonged periods. They respond to such exercise by becoming stronger and able to work hard for progressively greater lengths of time.

Flexibility The body's ability to move through a full *range of motion,* called FLEXIBILITY, is also an essential component of fitness. Anyone who has experienced stiff, tight muscles or a severe sprain knows how a restricted range of motion limits activity. Flexibility allows muscles and joints to move to their maximum extent, easing all movement and reducing the chances of injury. Flexibility is improved through STRETCHING EXERCISES that keep muscles supple and loose.

Body Composition An additional aspect of fitness is BODY COMPOSITION, the ratio of fat to bone and muscle in the body. The body composition of a fit person has the appropriate amount of body fat required to maintain good health. People who have higher percentages of their body weight constituted by fat should start a FITNESS TRAINING program, whether they are OVERWEIGHT or not.

In general, any exercise that improves strength and endurance is likely to improve body composition by adding to muscle mass and increasing energy expenditures. Burning more CALORIES than are consumed requires the body to convert its surplus fat in order to produce the additional energy required by the body. (See also SPORTS AND FITNESS; WEIGHT ASSESSMENT.)

Fitness and Aerobic Exercise.
Cardiovascular fitness and muscular endurance develop together as a result of aerobic exercise.

▶ **FITNESS TRAINING** Fitness training is physical conditioning intended to improve a person's overall level of FITNESS. It requires regular EXERCISE of the entire body with the goal of enhancing each of the elements of fitness: STRENGTH, ENDURANCE, FLEXIBILITY, and BODY COMPOSITION.

Planning a Fitness Program The particular nature of a fitness program depends on a person's level of fitness and individual goals. However, fitness training necessarily involves three major classes of exercise.

STRENGTH EXERCISE, such as WEIGHT TRAINING or working on EXERCISE MACHINES, is primarily intended to build *muscle strength.* Some types of strength exercise also strengthen bones, improve endurance, and, by adding muscle mass, enhance body composition.

Fitness Training. *To become fit, you must exercise frequently, with enough intensity, and for a sufficient time period.*

AEROBIC EXERCISE, such as RUNNING or AEROBIC DANCE, builds endurance by raising the HEART RATE for extended periods of time. It is of special benefit to the cardiovascular system. It can also increase muscle strength and, by burning calories rapidly, improve body composition.

STRETCHING EXERCISE is primarily intended to enhance flexibility by expanding the *range of motion* of joints and muscles. It also helps prevent injury when done before other forms of exercise, as well as soreness and stiffness when performed after an exercise session.

Achieving Fitness   Improving fitness takes time. When you begin a training program, you will probably feel sore and fatigued at first. Most people begin feeling more fit in 8 to 12 weeks; they find they can exercise harder, longer, and more easily than at the start. After 2 or 3 months of regular training, many reach a plateau and will have to work harder to improve aerobic capacity and strength. Keep in mind that if fitness training is stopped, fitness gains will be lost in about the same time it took to achieve them.

Achieving true fitness requires a commitment to regular exercise. Aerobic exercise, for example, requires three sessions of 20 to 30 minutes each week in order to be effective.

Benefits of Fitness Training   Being fit is a great benefit to your health. Fit people generally feel better, get fewer illnesses and diseases, and live longer. Fitness training has many other advantages, including improved appearance and self-image, extra energy and strength, and reduced fatigue and tension. (See also CROSS TRAINING; ENERGY, PHYSICAL; SPORTS AND FITNESS.)

▶ FIVE FOOD GROUPS SYSTEM

The five food groups system is a method for planning a balanced diet that divides food into five categories. Similar to the FOUR FOOD GROUPS SYSTEM, it adds a fifth group of "extra" foods that contain few NUTRIENTS. An awareness of the fifth food group can help people limit the less nutritious foods they eat.

How the System Works   The four basic food groups used in the system are:

- ▸ The BREADS AND CEREALS GROUP, which includes various grain products including bread, cereal, pasta, and rice
- ▸ The FRUITS AND VEGETABLES GROUP, which includes foods such as bananas, citrus fruits, potatoes, and broccoli
- ▸ The MEATS, EGGS, AND LEGUMES GROUP, which includes meats, poultry, eggs, and fish as well as peas, beans, and nuts
- ▸ The MILK AND MILK PRODUCTS GROUP, which includes dairy products such as milk, cheese, and yogurt

The five food groups system makes recommendations about how many daily servings from each food group make up a nutritious diet. Serving sizes are specified. A serving from the breads and cereals group, for example, would be one slice of bread; from the fruits and vegetables

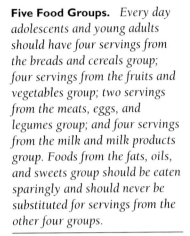

Five Food Groups. *Every day adolescents and young adults should have four servings from the breads and cereals group; four servings from the fruits and vegetables group; two servings from the meats, eggs, and legumes group; and four servings from the milk and milk products group. Foods from the fats, oils, and sweets group should be eaten sparingly and should never be substituted for servings from the other four groups.*

group, an orange; from the meats, eggs, and legumes group, 3 ounces (85 g) of cooked, lean meat; and from the milk and milk products group, 8 ounces (237 mL) of milk.

The number of daily servings recommended varies with a person's age. Adolescents and young adults should eat two servings from the meats group, and four servings from each of the other three groups, every day.

The fifth food group is called the FATS, OILS, AND SWEETS GROUP. It includes foods that are high in CALORIES but relatively low in nutrients. Examples of these are: butter, margarine, vegetable oil, sugar, honey, pastries and cakes, and soft drinks. These foods should be eaten in small amounts and should never take the place of servings from the other groups.

HEALTHY CHOICES

Using the System Thinking of fats and sugars as a group makes it easier to avoid eating them too frequently. A nutritious diet should be made up primarily of foods in the four other groups plus a limited consumption of fats, oils, and sweets. (See also DIETARY GUIDELINES; EXCHANGE SYSTEM; FOOD GROUP SYSTEMS; FOOD PYRAMID SYSTEM.)

▶ FLEXIBILITY

Flexibility is the ability of joints to move through a full range of motion. Flexibility, STRENGTH, and muscular and cardiovascular ENDURANCE are the basic elements of physical FITNESS. Flexibility is increased when muscles and other connective tissues that support the joints are developed and lengthened with regular STRETCHING EXERCISES. The elasticity of the connective tissue at each joint also determines flexibility.

Stretching Exercises. *There are many different ways to loosen up muscles.*

The maximum range of motion of body joints varies according to the type of joint. The knee, for example, has a more limited range of motion than the shoulder. However, the flexibility of all joints and muscles can be improved through regular EXERCISE.

Importance of Flexibility Improving flexibility protects against muscle pulls and tears. It also helps in the performance of everyday activities, contributing to better posture, more graceful movement, and fewer aches and pains in joints and muscles. Lower-back pain, for example, can often be reduced by exercises that increase the flexibility of thigh and lower-back muscles while strengthening the abdominal muscles.

Building Flexibility Stretching exercises are the main method of improving flexibility. When beginning a stretching program, exercise muscles slowly and steadily (see illustration: Stretching Exercises). Maintain a regular routine that progresses gradually. Do not stretch muscles to the point of feeling pain. (See also FITNESS TRAINING; SPORTS INJURIES; STRENGTH EXERCISE.)

► FOOD ADDITIVES

Food additives are chemical substances added to foods for a variety of purposes. These include preserving food so it will keep its appearance and freshness longer, boosting nutritional value, improving taste and texture, and adding desired color. In the United States, the Food and Drug Administration regulates the use of food additives and has approved about 3,000 different natural and synthetic materials used in food preparation.

Preservatives Preservatives are chemicals called *antimicrobials* that resist the growth of harmful organisms and chemicals called *antioxidants* that slow down changes in food color and flavor caused by exposure to air. The most familiar and widely used antimicrobials are SALT and SUGAR. Salt is used to preserve meat and fish, and sugar is used in jam and jelly. Other chemicals used as antimicrobials are sodium propionate, used to keep bread and other baked goods fresh; calcium sorbate, which is added to processed cheeses, syrups, mayonnaise, and margarine; and nitrites, which are used to protect hot dogs and other cured meats from dangerous bacteria, including the organism that causes *botulism*. Common antioxidants are *vitamin C* (ascorbic acid), added to fruit products and acidic foods; propyl gallate, used in cereals, snack foods, and pastries; and *vitamin E*, used in oils and shortenings.

Nutrition Boosters NUTRIENTS are added to some foods to improve the nutritional value. Examples of enriched (or fortified) foods include salt (with added iodine), dairy products (vitamin A and vitamin D), and cereals (various vitamins and minerals).

Flavoring Agents Flavoring agents are used in food to enhance or change flavor. ARTIFICIAL SWEETENERS such as aspartame are used to sweeten many different diet foods. MONOSODIUM GLUTAMATE (MSG), although having no taste of its own, is used to enhance the flavor of foods.

Emulsifiers Emulsifiers are used to achieve desired consistencies of foods. Examples include carob bean gum, the thickening agent that gives ice cream its rich texture, and lecithin, which is used in mayonnaise and peanut butter.

Coloring Agents Coloring agents are used to improve the appearance of foods as well as many drugs and cosmetics. Examples include annatto extract, a yellowish-red food dye used in cheeses, and tartrazine, a yellow dye used in many drinks, cake mixes, cheese foods, and candy.

RISK FACTORS
▶ ▶ ▶ ▶ ▶ ▶

The use of additives in foods and beverages is controversial. Certain additives, most notably MSG and the coloring agent tartrazine, can provoke physical reactions in people with sensitivities or allergies to these chemicals. Reactions include headaches, rashes, difficulty breathing, and fainting. The role of additives in causing certain kinds of cancers is also the subject of debate and research. The nitrites used in hot dogs, sandwich meats, and bacon are of particular concern.

Given these problems, some consumers argue that additives should not be used. But most food additives serve necessary functions. They make foods safer, more nutritious, and more palatable. In the case of preservatives, the risk of bacteria contamination outweighs any health risks from the chemical preservative. The necessity of food coloring, however, may be less sound, because these agents are used for purely cosmetic reasons.

The FDA attempts to minimize the risks to the food supply from additives by requiring thorough testing of any new additives and periodically reviewing additives that have already been approved. Still, it is your responsibility to know the contents of the foods you eat and, if you are subject to allergies, to avoid those additives that cause physical reactions. (See also FOOD ALLERGIES; FOOD LABELING; FOOD PRESERVATION METHODS; FOOD SAFETY; ORGANIC FOOD; FOOD AND DRUG ADMINISTRATION, **7.**)

▶ **FOOD ALLERGIES** Food allergies are abnormal reactions to food caused by an *antibody response*. An allergic reaction occurs when the body reacts to a specific food by producing antibodies. The antibodies release substances (called *histamines*) that irritate the body tissues, producing a range of symptoms, some potentially life-threatening. (See also ANTIBODY, **2.**)

Symptoms of Food Allergies In most cases, the symptoms of food allergies are simply unpleasant. They include abdominal pain, vomiting, nausea, diarrhea, hives, eczema, fainting, nasal congestion, sneezing, and swelling of the lips, tongue, throat, eyes, and face.

The most severe form of allergic reaction to food is *anaphylactic shock*, a sudden severe loss of blood pressure and collapse of the cardiovascular system. Anaphylactic shock requires immediate emergency medical treatment. (See also ANAPHYLACTIC SHOCK, **8.**)

Common Food Allergies Foods that most often trigger allergic reactions include milk, eggs, berries, soybeans, shellfish, wheat, corn, nuts, and beans. A few FOOD ADDITIVES may also trigger allergies.

Many young children develop food allergies, but they often outgrow them by age 6. Adults with food allergies usually suffer from other allergic conditions, such as asthma or hay fever.

How to Identify Food Allergies Some food allergies cause an immediate reaction, making them easy to identify. However, other foods can take hours or days to cause a reaction and are therefore not easy to pinpoint. Physicians diagnose these food allergies by taking an extensive personal history and by performing a variety of tests. If a specific food allergy cannot be identified, a physician may prescribe antihistamines or other drugs to relieve the symptoms. (See also ANTIHISTAMINES AND DECONGESTANTS, 7.)

Many people believe they have food allergies when, in fact, other problems, such as stress or *food intolerance,* are responsible for causing discomfort. Emotional and physical stresses can greatly impair the digestion of food, causing symptoms similar to those produced by food allergies. Food intolerance also causes unpleasant reactions to food. People with a food intolerance are unable to digest the food or a component of it because they lack certain enzymes (chemicals that help speed up certain processes in the body). For example, many people have *lactose intolerance,* the inability to digest the sugar in milk.

How to Prevent Food Allergies The only way to prevent food allergies is to avoid the foods that trigger a reaction. People who must restrict their DIETS because of allergies should make sure that they are still eating a balanced diet. (See also ALLERGIES, 3.)

Food Allergy. *Sensitivity to cow's milk is a common food allergy, especially in young children.*

▶ FOOD CRAVING

A food craving is a strong desire to eat a certain food. Researchers are not quite sure why food cravings occur, but many believe that they are caused by both physiological and psychological factors. Whatever their sources, food cravings are sometimes powerful enough to produce episodes of compulsive overeating in some people.

Physiological Cravings A physiological craving reflects a physical need for a food. A craving for foods high in CARBOHYDRATES has been noted in people who exercise heavily, for example. This craving may come from the lowered blood sugar levels resulting from exercise, a condition best remedied by carbohydrate consumption. Some cravings seem to be associated with natural bodily rhythms, such as the menstrual cycle. For example, some women crave carbohydrate foods after they ovulate and may eat as many as 500 extra calories a day before menstruation. These extra calories may be needed to make the uterus ready for pregnancy. Cravings for salty foods during pregnancy are also common and are explained by the body's increased need for SODIUM during pregnancy. Other cravings may have evolved to protect the species. Many people tend to eat foods richer in fat during the fall and winter months. This increased calorie intake may result from the historical necessity for human beings to stay warm in cold weather—a great survival benefit when they faced long periods of exposure to cold. Most Americans, however, now

Psychological Cravings. *Some cravings are extremely strong and can be made worse by a rigid, strict diet.*

spend most of the cold months in warmly heated buildings, though they may still experience such cravings.

Psychological Cravings   A psychological craving is a strong desire for a particular food in the absence of a physical need for the food. The sources of psychological cravings for specific foods are not well understood. Most likely, they result from associations—conscious or subconscious—of foods with pleasant experiences or sensations in a person's past. For example, the feelings of comfort provided by foods such as ice cream or cookies that were given as rewards during childhood could explain cravings for those foods. A strict diet may also result in psychological cravings.

HEALTHY CHOICES

Coping with Food Craving   Many nutrition experts think that understanding the basis of food cravings can help people keep them under control. Moderation in eating desired foods, rather than total denial, is recommended as a way to avoid cravings that can result in overeating. (See also APPETITE; WEIGHT MANAGEMENT.)

▶ **FOOD ENERGY**   see ENERGY, FOOD

▶ **FOOD GROUP SYSTEMS**   Food group systems place foods in categories in order to simplify the task of diet planning. Ensuring a well-balanced diet with adequate NUTRIENTS—PROTEINS, CARBOHYDRATES, FATS, VITAMINS, and MINERALS—can seem very complex. Every food contains different amounts of different nutrients. But certain foods have basic nutritional similarities that are the basis of the categorization schemes of food group systems.

Grouping foods according to what they have in common makes planning for good nutrition much easier. For example, vitamins A and C are important for good health, and they are most commonly found in fruits and vegetables. Fruits and vegetables make up one food group in several food group systems. In addition to their high vitamin content, fruits and vegetables share the fact that they are relatively low in CALORIES, very low in fat, and high in FIBER. Meat and eggs are often similarly grouped because they are good sources of protein, although relatively high in CHOLESTEROL and saturated fat. Similarities such as these are used to define specific *food groups* in all of the familiar classification systems.

Nutritionists have developed several food group systems, each with different goals. Each system suggests eating particular numbers of servings or amounts from the food groups it includes. The goal of all the systems is to ensure that a person's diet includes all the key nutrients in appropriate quantities. The FOUR FOOD GROUPS SYSTEM, the FIVE FOOD GROUPS SYSTEM, and the FOOD PYRAMID SYSTEM group foods by their basic nutritional components. The EXCHANGE SYSTEM further distinguishes foods by their calorie content as well as by amounts of various nutrients. (See also BREADS AND CEREALS GROUP; DIETARY GUIDELINES; FATS, OILS, AND SWEETS GROUP; FRUITS AND VEGETABLES GROUP; MEATS, EGGS, AND LEGUMES GROUP; MILK AND MILK PRODUCTS GROUP.)

> The goal of all the food group systems is to ensure that a person's diet includes all the key nutrients in appropriate quantities.

► FOOD LABELING

Food labeling is the listing of important information about the content of a food product on the outside of its package. By federal law, all food labels must include the name of the product, the net contents or net weight of the package, and the name or location of the manufacturer, packer, or distributor. In addition, some labels list the ingredients, show information about the NUTRIENTS, and provide a freshness date.

List of Ingredients   Labels for most foods must also contain a list of all ingredients and any FOOD ADDITIVES. The ingredients must be listed on the label in descending order based on weight. For example, if a cereal package lists its ingredients as "sugar, corn, salt, and malt flavoring," then it contains more sugar than any other ingredient.

Nutrition Labeling   When a manufacturer adds a nutrient to a food or makes a claim about it, such as that it is "low-fat" or "low-calorie," the package must also include nutrition labeling.

Nutritional information is usually shown in two parts. The first lists the serving size, the number of CALORIES, and, by weight, the amount of PROTEIN, CARBOHYDRATES, FAT, and SODIUM in the food. Many labels also include the amount of CHOLESTEROL and POTASSIUM.

The second part of a food's nutrition label lists the amount of protein and seven essential VITAMINS and MINERALS contained in one serving as a percentage of their RECOMMENDED DIETARY ALLOWANCE (RDA). If a label says that one serving provides 25 percent of the RDA of vitamin C, that means it provides one-fourth of the daily amount of vitamin C required by the average adult. The *Food and Nutrition Board* of the National Academy of Sciences establishes RDAs.

```
NUTRITION INFORMATION PER SERVING
SERVING SIZE ........................ 9¹/₂ OZ. (269 g)
SERVINGS PER CONTAINER ......................... 2
CALORIES ..................................................... 150
PROTEIN (GRAMS) ........................................... 4
CARBOHYDRATE (GRAMS) ............................ 25
FAT (GRAMS) .................................................... 4
SODIUM ........................................ 950 mg/serving

PERCENTAGE OF U.S. RECOMMENDED
DIETARY ALLOWANCES (U.S. RDA)
PROTEIN ................. 6      VITAMIN C ............ 4
RIBOFLAVIN .......... 4      CALCIUM ............. 6
VITAMIN A .......... 110      THIAMINE ............ 4
NIACIN .................... 8      IRON ................... 10
```

Food Label. *The first part of a nutrition label contains nutritional information for each serving, including the amount of calories, protein, carbohydrates, fat, and sodium. The second part contains the percentage of U.S. recommended dietary allowances for protein and seven essential vitamins and minerals.*

Federal law forbids manufacturers from making certain misleading nutritional claims on labels. It also requires the use of specific terms in some cases (*imitation,* for example) and quantitatively defines the meaning of others (such as *sodium-free*).

Food Product Dating   Food product dating, which is generally not required by law, indicates how long a product will remain fresh and wholesome. A packaged food may be labeled by a sell or pull date, which is the last date the store should sell it. Foods such as meat and milk usually remain fresh for several days after the indicated date. A package may also have an expiration or freshness date that indicates the last date that a product should be used.

Regulating Labeling   The *Food and Drug Administration* (FDA) is the federal agency responsible for regulating food labeling. In 1992, the FDA approved significant new restrictions to control the use of misleading information and claims on food labels. The new regulations focus on the nutritional needs of an average American and also standardize serving sizes. In addition, they establish standard definitions for terms such as *light* and *low-fat.* They also require nutrition labeling for most processed foods and, for the first time, for some fresh, unprocessed foods. The new regulations also require that any health claims made by manufacturers be supported by scientific evidence. (See also DIETARY GUIDELINES; FOOD AND DRUG ADMINISTRATION, 7.)

▷ **FOOD POISONING**   Food poisoning is gastrointestinal illness caused by eating contaminated food. Food can be contaminated by a variety of microorganisms, including bacteria, viruses, yeast, and molds. Food-poisoning symptoms include loss of appetite, nausea, vomiting, diarrhea, and stomachache. Symptoms usually pass within a few hours.

Bacterial Food Poisoning   Most food poisoning is caused by *bacteria.* The most common is caused by *Staphylococcus aureus* bacteria. These bacteria can spread by sneezing or coughing on food or from an open wound on the hand of a food preparer. Symptoms of *staph infection* appear within 3 to 6 hours after eating contaminated food and last for about 12 hours. *Clostridium perfringens* bacteria may contaminate cooked meat that is allowed to stand for several hours at room temperature. *Salmonella* food poisoning can be life-threatening to infants and elderly people. About 12 to 48 hours after eating food contaminated with salmonella, typical food-poisoning symptoms appear and may be accompanied by a fever. Salmonella are often found in poultry, eggs, and meat. Cooking these foods thoroughly destroys these bacteria.

Botulism is a rare but very dangerous type of food poisoning. It occurs when bacteria multiply in sealed containers of food that have been processed at temperatures that are too low. The bacteria that cause botulism (*Clostridium botulinum*) produce a *toxin* that cannot be destroyed by heating the food before eating it. If a can is swollen or leaking or if the safety button on a jar lid has popped up, the container may be

Safe Food-Handling Practices.
In an unclean kitchen, food can easily become contaminated and cause food poisoning.

contaminated and should be returned to its place of purchase. Symptoms of botulism include muscle weakness and double vision in addition to typical food-poisoning symptoms. It is potentially fatal and must be treated immediately.

Traveler's diarrhea is caused most often by drinking water or eating foods contaminated with the common intestinal bacterium *Escherichia coli*. It causes severe diarrhea that can last several days. When traveling abroad, avoid untreated water, salads, uncooked milk products, and raw fruits and vegetables that you cannot peel, unless you are sure they are safe.

Other Sources of Food Poisoning   Food poisoning can also result from eating contaminated or spoiled seafood. For example, the *hepatitis virus* can be spread by eating raw shellfish from waters contaminated with sewage. Some foods can also be contaminated by *parasites*. Certain other foods, including peanuts, potatoes, and some wild mushrooms, can produce toxins that can cause illness. Occasionally, *insecticide* or *pesticide* residue on foods can create food-poisoning symptoms.

Prevention   In most cases, however, food poisoning is the result of unsafe food-handling practices. Many cases of food poisoning can be prevented by following basic FOOD SAFETY guidelines: Clean all food preparation areas with hot, soapy water, cook foods at temperatures high enough to kill bacteria, and cool and refrigerate foods promptly. (See also BACTERIAL INFECTIONS, **2**; DIARRHEA, **2**; PARASITIC INFECTIONS, **2**; SALMONELLA INFECTIONS, **2**; VIRAL INFECTIONS, **2**; VOMITING, **2**.)

► FOOD PRESERVATION METHODS

Food preservation methods slow the spoiling process of food. All foods eventually spoil, but preservation keeps food fresh so it can be shipped long distances, eaten out of season, and stored for long periods in case of shortages. This reduces waste and helps to ensure a steady food supply. In addition, food preservation prevents illnesses caused by bacteria and other microorganisms and increases the quality and variety of food available.

How Food Spoils *Enzymes* in foods such as fruits cause them to ripen. But as the action of enzymes continues, the food eventually spoils. *Microorganisms,* including molds, yeasts, and bacteria, cause changes in food that may give it an unpleasant taste or odor. They may also produce harmful substances in the food.

Many methods of food preservation have been developed over the years. Some have been around for centuries, while others use new technology. Food preservation methods include drying, pasteurization, canning, refrigeration, freezing, chemical preservation, and irradiation.

Methods Using Heat *Drying,* one of the oldest methods of food preservation, uses heat. Food can be dried in the sunlight or by special machinery that circulates hot air to remove moisture from food. Both methods remove water from the food so that enzymes and microorganisms cannot survive. Fruits, peas, beans, meat, fish, and milk are just a few of the many foods that can be dried.

Pasteurization (a process invented by and named after French chemist Louis Pasteur) is used to preserve liquids such as milk and juice. The liquid is heated, which destroys many of the organisms in milk that cause spoilage. The food will stay fresh longer but will spoil eventually. This is why even pasteurized milk is kept in the refrigerator. *Sterilization* is a process in which foods are heated to even higher temperatures, destroying all microorganisms and preventing spoiling.

Canning is another heating process that keeps food fresh. Foods are sealed in metal or glass containers before they are heated.

> The temperature in a refrigerator is just above freezing. This slows the growth of bacteria and molds in many foods but does not stop it entirely.

Methods Using Cold Cold temperatures can also be used to preserve food. Many foods are shipped to markets in refrigerated ships, trucks, or trains. At the store, the food is kept in refrigerated cases. The temperature in *refrigerators* is just above freezing. This dramatically slows the growth of bacteria and molds in many foods, but does not stop it entirely.

Freezing is another method of preserving food with cold temperatures. Keeping food at extremely cold temperatures greatly slows the growth of microorganisms and enzyme activity. Frozen foods will last a long time but not indefinitely.

Freeze-drying is a process that preserves food by first freezing it. The frozen food is then placed in a vacuum tank to remove the water, leaving a dry, spongelike solid. Freeze-dried foods keep their flavor and texture better than do foods preserved by drying. Instant coffee and soup mixes are sometimes prepared this way.

Chemical Preservation For centuries, people have added substances to food to preserve it. *Salt* can keep meat and fish from spoiling. *Sugar* is used as a preservative in jams and jellies. Ham and bacon are preserved, or *cured,* with a combination of salt and wood smoke. Vinegar used in the *pickling* process preserves pickles and other foods. Many FOOD ADDITIVES are used in food processing as preservatives, as well as to improve taste and color.

Irradiation   Irradiating food destroys microorganisms and insects. It also prevents new shoots from sprouting on potatoes and onions. The technology for irradiation is relatively new, and guidelines for its use have recently been set by the U.S. Food and Drug Administration. Irradiation can help to preserve many foods with little or no change in taste or texture. When exposed to radiation, the food does not become radioactive. There remains some concern, however, over possible health risks.

One of the benefits of food preservation is that it reduces the risk of illness caused by spoiled food. But food preservation methods themselves may carry risks. Some scientists believe that not enough is known about certain food additives and irradiation. Researchers continue to study these and other food preservation methods to make sure that they are safe. (See also FOOD SAFETY; FOOD AND DRUG ADMINISTRATION, 7.)

▶ **FOOD PYRAMID SYSTEM**   The food pyramid system is a method of planning for a balanced diet. It uses a pyramid-shaped diagram to show the quantities that should be consumed daily from a number of food groups. The pyramid is a helpful way of depicting nutrition because it is a graphic representation of the proportions contributed by each food group to a balanced diet.

How the Pyramid Works   The food pyramid system was developed by the U.S. Department of Agriculture (USDA). It divides foods into six basic groups. These are roughly equivalent to the categories of the FIVE FOOD GROUPS SYSTEM, with the exception that the FRUITS AND VEGETABLES GROUP becomes two separate groups in the pyramid system. The six groups constitute a four-tiered triangle, which is meant to indicate the relative quantities to be consumed from each group. The group at the pyramid's broad base (bread, rice, cereal, and pasta, or simply the BREADS AND CEREALS GROUP) is recommended as the largest source of CALORIES in the diet. The FATS, OILS, AND SWEETS GROUP lies at the top of the pyramid, an indication of the small quantities of foods recommended for consumption from this group. Food groups at the broad base of the pyramid are meant to be eaten in greater quantities than are those at the narrow top of the pyramid. Foods in the middle of the pyramid should be eaten in moderate amounts.

> Food groups at the broad base of the pyramid are meant to be eaten in greater quantities than those at the narrow top of the pyramid.

Using the System   Recommended daily quantities of each type of food are indicated on the food pyramid. They are usually expressed as a number of servings per day. There is often a range in the serving amounts, for example: bread, rice, cereal, pasta, 6 to 11 servings daily. This is because nutritional needs vary according to age and level of activity. The lower amount is for people who are less active and need fewer calories every

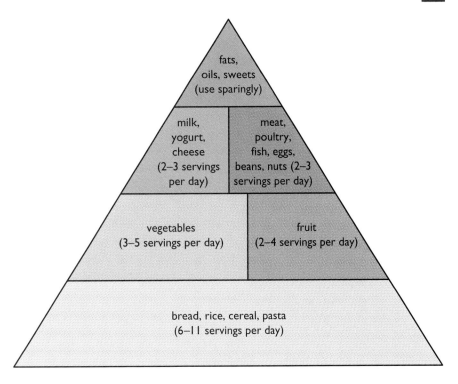

Food Pyramid. *The USDA's food pyramid is one way to understand the elements that go into a balanced diet. Foods that are at the broad base of the pyramid should form the largest part of your diet. Recommended servings per day vary with the age and activity level of the individual.*

day. The higher amount is for active people or young people, who need more calories.

When it was first announced, the USDA's food pyramid system generated some controversy. Some groups, especially representatives of the meat and dairy industries, objected to the small amount of space devoted to their products. They were also concerned that the placement of these foods near fats, oils, and sweets implied that meat and dairy products were harmful rather than beneficial. Others felt that placing fats, oils, and sweets at the top of the pyramid created the mistaken impression that these are desirable foods.

The food pyramid, however, is just another way of presenting familiar advice: A nutritious diet should include more servings of grains, fruits, and vegetables than of meats and dairy products. Fats, oils, and sweets should make up a very small part of a well-balanced diet. The pyramid's advantage is that it reminds people at a glance which foods to focus on, which to eat sparingly, and how to balance the foods they eat to maintain good health. (See also DIETARY GUIDELINES; EXCHANGE SYSTEM; FOOD GROUP SYSTEMS; FOUR FOOD GROUPS SYSTEM; MEATS, EGGS, AND LEGUMES GROUP; MILK AND MILK PRODUCTS GROUP; NUTRIENTS.)

HEALTHY CHOICES

► FOOD SAFETY

Food safety refers to the principles and practices for keeping foods free from the dangers of spoilage and contamination. For commercial food suppliers and public eating places, federal, state, and local health departments provide regulations for storing, preparing, and serving foods and conduct inspections to ensure food safety. By following the same principles

Using a Meat Thermometer.
It is important to cook meat thoroughly to prevent food poisoning. A meat thermometer should be used to tell when the meat is ready. For best results, place the thermometer in the thickest part of the meat and make sure that it is not touching a bone.

at home, you can help prevent FOOD POISONING, a gastrointestinal illness that results from eating spoiled or contaminated food.

HEALTHY CHOICES

Keep Your Hands and Food Preparation Areas Clean   Cleanliness around food is very important in order to avoid *bacterial contamination.* Wash your hands with soap and water before and after handling food, after using the bathroom, after touching pets, and after blowing your nose or touching your mouth. Use a clean spoon to taste-test foods. Try to avoid preparing food if you are ill, and wear rubber gloves if you have an infected cut on your hand.

Wash utensils, cutting boards, dishes, and the sink in hot, soapy water. Use clean dishcloths and dish towels for every meal, and wash sponges after each use and allow them to dry.

Prepare and Cook Foods Carefully   Many common foods normally carry bacteria. Always wash fruits and vegetables carefully to remove excess bacteria and pesticides that may be on the surface.

Meats, poultry, and fish require special handling. Do not allow these foods to thaw at room temperature. Instead, use a microwave oven, or thaw items in the refrigerator and then cook immediately. Wash the cutting board and knife in hot, soapy water and rinse with very hot water. You may want to reserve a cutting board for meat, fish, and poultry only. If you marinate meat or poultry and want to serve the juices, boil them for several minutes first. Use a clean plate and utensil when serving the cooked food so that it will not be contaminated by its raw juices.

Use a meat thermometer when cooking poultry and pork (see illustration: Using a Meat Thermometer). Poultry should be cooked until the thermometer registers 180 to 185°F (82.2 to 84.9°C); pork should be cooked until the temperature reaches 137°F (58.3°C). Also check the meat's juices. When the meat is thoroughly cooked, the juices will run clear.

Contamination of eggs with *Salmonella* bacteria is a growing concern. Discard cracked eggs, and cook eggs thoroughly to destroy any bacteria. Also, avoid dishes that contain raw eggs, such as hollandaise sauce, homemade eggnog, and Caesar salad dressing.

When canning vegetables at home, follow reliable instructions, such as those provided by the U.S. Department of Agriculture, and use the pressure-canner method of canning.

Store Foods Correctly   Many foods are perishable, or liable to spoil. Use *perishable foods* quickly, and refrigerate or freeze leftovers immediately. The freezer must be kept at 0°F (−17.7°C), and the refrigerator temperature should be between 36 and 40°F (2.2 and 4.4°C) to maintain the quality of food. Allowing cooked food to sit at room temperature is dangerous. It can take as little as 4 hours for bacteria to multiply enough to cause food poisoning. Turkey or chicken stuffing should be removed from the bird and refrigerated separately.

Store foods such as sugar, cereals, flour, and packaged mixes in containers with snug-fitting lids to avoid *contamination by insects and rodents*. Some whole-grain products, for example, wheat germ and whole-wheat flour, can spoil at room temperature. Refrigeration or freezing is necessary to keep them fresh.

Make refrigerator cleanup a regular task. Dispose of food that has been stored too long, especially if it has become moldy. Hard cheeses with mold are safe to eat, however, if you trim the mold away.

Purchase Foods with Care   When purchasing food, look closely at how well it is stored in the grocery. Do not buy foods stored above the frostline in the grocery freezer. If you are buying foods from a salad bar, make sure the items are sufficiently chilled and protected from the coughs and sneezes of other customers. Never buy canned food if the cans are bulging or if the safety button on the lid has popped up. These are signs of botulism contamination, a dangerous type of food poisoning. Do not use this food. Instead, return it to its place of purchase (see illustration: Signs of Botulism Contamination). Buy fish from a reliable merchant who sells fresh fish and is knowledgeable about its sources.

Some foods naturally contain harmful substances. The sprouts, eyes, and green parts of a potato can make you sick. Certain wild mushrooms can also cause serious illness or death, so be sure of the origin and safety of the food you prepare.

Many packaged foods and beverages contain chemical *preservatives* to prevent spoilage. Some people have a sensitivity to these FOOD ADDITIVES and experience unpleasant symptoms after eating food containing them. If you have this problem, read labels carefully and avoid foods with preservatives. (See also FOOD ALLERGIES; FOOD LABELING; BACTERIAL INFECTIONS, **2**; SALMONELLA INFECTIONS, **2**.)

Signs of Botulism Contamination. *Do not use a can of food if it is bulging or leaking or if the safety button has popped up.*

▷ **FOUR FOOD GROUPS SYSTEM** The four food groups system (or Basic Four System) is a method of nutritional planning that divides foods into four categories according to the kinds of NUTRIENTS they supply. It also specifies the number of servings that should be chosen from each food group daily. A person can use the system to ensure a balanced diet by eating the recommended servings from each group.

How the System Works The four basic food groups used in the system are:

- The BREADS AND CEREALS GROUP, which includes various grain products including bread, cereal, pasta, and rice
- The FRUITS AND VEGETABLES GROUP, which includes foods such as apples, citrus fruits, spinach, and carrots
- The MEATS, EGGS, AND LEGUMES GROUP, which includes meats, poultry, eggs, and fish as well as peas, beans, and nuts
- The MILK AND MILK PRODUCTS GROUP, which includes dairy products such as milk, cheese, and yogurt

The system recommends eating a certain number of daily servings of specified size from each food group. A serving from the breads and cereals group, for example, would be one slice of bread; from the fruits and vegetables group, an apple; from the meats, eggs, and legumes group, 3 ounces (85 g) of cooked, lean meat; and from the milk and milk products group, 8 ounces (237 mL) of milk.

The number of daily servings recommended varies with a person's age. Everyone should eat at least four servings daily from the breads and cereals group, four servings from the fruits and vegetables group, and two

THE FOUR FOOD GROUPS		
Food group	**Minimum number of daily servings**	**Sample servings**
Breads and cereals	4 for all ages	1 slice bread 1 oz (28 g) ready-to-eat cereal ½ cup (118 mL) pasta or rice
Fruits and vegetables	4 for all ages	½ cup (118 mL) juice 1 medium apple, banana, or orange ½ cup (118 mL) vegetables
Meats, eggs, and legumes	2 for all ages	2–3 oz (57–85 g) cooked, lean meat, fish, or poultry 1 egg 2 tbsp (30 mL) peanut butter ½ cup (118 mL) cooked dried peas or dried beans
Milk and milk products	2 for adults 3 for children 4 for teenagers and young adults	1 cup (237 mL) milk 1 cup (237 mL) yogurt 1 oz (28 g) cheese

Source: Guide to good eating, 5th ed. Courtesy National Dairy Council®.

servings from the meats, eggs, and legumes group. Adolescents and young adults should eat four servings from the milk and milk products group, children should eat three servings, and everyone else should eat two servings (see chart: The Four Food Groups).

Some things you eat are made up of a combination of foods from different food groups. Sandwiches, pizza, and lasagna are examples of such foods. These foods are counted as servings (or partial servings) of the groups from which they are made. This system also recognizes a category of foods called "Others." These foods are usually high in CALORIES but low in nutrients. Potato chips, cookies, and soft drinks are in this category. These foods should be eaten sparingly.

HEALTHY CHOICES

Using the System   A healthful diet should include a wide variety of foods from each of the four food groups. Not all foods in a group supply nutrients in exactly the same amounts. Some foods are good sources of more than one nutrient. Eating the recommended number of servings of foods from all four groups, and varying the kinds of foods eaten within each group, will help maintain a healthy, well-balanced diet. (See also DI-ETARY GUIDELINES; EXCHANGE SYSTEM; FIVE FOOD GROUPS SYSTEM; FOOD GROUP SYSTEMS; FOOD PYRAMID SYSTEM.)

FRUITS AND VEGETABLES GROUP   The fruits and vegetables food group is a class of foods made up of the edible parts—whether roots, leaves, shoots, or flesh—of a variety of plants. This group includes foods such as apples, oranges, bananas, melons, spinach, carrots, and squash. On the whole, fruits are sweeter than vegetables. Both, however, are important sources of NUTRIENTS such as CARBOHYDRATES, VITAMINS, and MINERALS. All fruits and most vegetables may be eaten raw, but they may also be cooked before they are eaten. Some cooking methods, however, will significantly reduce their nutritive value.

Nutrition from Fruits and Vegetables   Both fruits and vegetables are made up largely of carbohydrates (including STARCH, SUGAR, and FIBER) and WATER. Most contain small amounts of PROTEIN and little or no FAT, although a few (avocado, for example) are high in fat. Most are low in CALORIES. Fruits and vegetables are rich sources of many vitamins and minerals. For example, dark yellow and dark green fruits and vegetables are high in BETA CAROTENE and VITAMIN A. These include apricots, carrots, cantaloupes, and spinach. Citrus fruits, such as oranges and grapefruit, as well as tomatoes, are excellent sources of VITAMIN C. Many fruits and vegetables provide CALCIUM, IRON, and POTASSIUM. Fruits and vegetables are also good sources of fiber, a substance that helps move food through the digestive tract.

Fruits and many vegetables are best eaten fresh and raw, because they lose vitamin content during storage and cooking. Avoid peeling edible skin such as that on apples and potatoes; this skin often contains the richest concentration of nutrients. Vegetables and fruits are also available frozen or canned. Steaming vegetables or cooking them in small amounts

Fruits and Vegetables Group.
Fruits and vegetables are rich in nutrients such as carbohydrates, vitamins, and minerals.

of water retains their nutrients better than boiling or frying. Cooking vegetables using a little water in a microwave oven will also retain most of their nutrients. Many fruits and vegetables, including apples, potatoes, and squash, can be baked or roasted to prevent a great loss of nutrients.

Daily Servings of Fruits and Vegetables Some FOOD GROUP SYSTEMS place fruits and vegetables together as a single food group; others list them separately. Most systems recommend at least four servings of fruits and vegetables each day, including at least one serving high in vitamin C. Most Americans do not eat as many fruits and vegetables as nutritionists recommend. Substituting these foods for other less nutritious ones in your diet will promote good health. (See also BREADS AND CEREALS GROUP; DIETARY GUIDELINES; EXCHANGE SYSTEM; FATS, OILS, AND SWEETS GROUP; FIVE FOOD GROUPS SYSTEM; FOOD PYRAMID SYSTEM; FOUR FOOD GROUPS SYSTEM; MEATS, EGGS, AND LEGUMES GROUP; MILK AND MILK PRODUCTS GROUP.)

HEALTHY CHOICES

▶ **GLUCOSE**

Glucose is a carbohydrate that the body needs for energy. It is one of the basic fuels for all living cells. Although some foods contain small amounts of glucose, the body produces most of it from other CARBOHYDRATES such as STARCHES and other SUGARS. These are reduced to glucose by the digestive process.

Glucose's Function Glucose has a simple chemical structure. It is absorbed directly into the bloodstream and carried to the cells. The cells then burn (or oxidize) the glucose to produce energy. This process is called *metabolism.*

Any unneeded glucose is converted to glycogen and stored in the liver and muscle tissues for later use. The glycogen can then be released for conversion into glucose any time the body needs more energy. (See also LIVER, **1**.)

Glucose. *Glucose is a unit making up starches in fruits, vegetables, and grains and is essential to body cells for energy.*

Blood Sugar Level Regardless of how many carbohydrates a person consumes, the amount of glucose in the blood, or the blood sugar level, is usually kept within narrow limits. Several hormones help maintain these limits. For example, if the blood sugar level gets too high, the *pancreas*, a large gland, releases the hormone *insulin*. Insulin enables the cells to take in more glucose and thus lowers the blood sugar level. (See also PANCREAS, 1; INSULIN, 7.)

Conversely, when the blood sugar level is too low, the pancreas releases the hormone glucagon. Glucagon stimulates the conversion of glycogen in the liver into glucose, which is then released into the blood. This raises the blood sugar level.

Blood Sugar Problems Sometimes people have problems with their blood sugar level. For example, people may have too much sugar in the blood, a condition known as *hyperglycemia.* Symptoms include frequent urination, extreme thirst, and glucose in the urine. People who have chronic hyperglycemia have a disease known as diabetes. Most people with diabetes have difficulty in taking up glucose from the blood. (See also DIABETES, 3.)

Hypoglycemia is the reverse of hyperglycemia. People with hypoglycemia do not have enough sugar in the blood. Symptoms include hunger, weakness, sweating, and dizziness.

People sometimes have minor, temporary attacks of hypoglycemia when they skip meals or eat meals that are high in carbohydrates. Eating regular meals, snacking between meals, and eating a normal amount of carbohydrates usually alleviates the condition. A physician should be consulted if any of these symptoms persist for a long time. (See also BODY METABOLISM; DIGESTION; ENERGY, FOOD; ENERGY, PHYSICAL.)

CONSULT A PHYSICIAN

▶ **GRAINS**   **see BREADS AND CEREALS GROUP**

▶ HEART RATE

Fitness and Heart Rate.
Trained athletes may have resting heart rates as low as 40 beats per minute.

Heart rate is the number of times the heart beats each minute. The rate increases while a person exercises and decreases while a person rests. Heart rate is an involuntary action, which means that a person cannot control it. However, heart rate can be beneficially lowered by regular EXERCISE.

Heart rate can be measured by taking the pulse. You need to place the tips of your index and middle fingers along the line of the radial artery, on the thumb side of the wrist or in the front of the neck under the jaw. Use a watch with a second hand to count the pulse for 10 seconds. Then multiply this count by 6. This gives the total number of heartbeats per minute.

Resting, Maximum, and Target Heart Rates   The range for *resting heart rate* for an adult is between 40 and 80 beats per minute. People with high *cardiovascular fitness* can pump more blood with each heartbeat; therefore, they tend to have heart rates on the low side of the normal range. People who are out of shape, however, typically have resting heart rates as high as 80 beats per minute or more. People who are unfit when they begin an exercise program will see their resting heart rates drop—perhaps as much as 10 to 15 beats per minute.

The oxygen demands of intensive exercise require the heart to work harder and can greatly speed the heart rate. There are limits, however, to how fast the heart can beat. *Maximum heart rate* varies from person to person and gradually decreases with age. Maximum heart rate can be estimated by subtracting a person's age from 220. For example, a 20-year-old would have a maximum heart rate of 200 beats per minute (220–20=200).

Like all muscles, the heart grows stronger in response to significant levels of regular work. *Target heart rate* is a scientific way of determining the amount of exercise necessary to increase cardiovascular ENDURANCE and achieve other health benefits of AEROBIC EXERCISE safely. This target rate is between 60 and 75 percent of maximum heart rate. For example, a 20-year-old person with a maximum heart rate of 200 will be exercising aerobically when the heart rate is between 120 (200 × 0.60) and 150 (200 × 0.75). A heart rate above 150 may indicate that a person who is just beginning an exercise program is exercising too vigorously. Below 120, the heart is not being required to work enough to achieve a significant benefit. For optimum results, you should do 20 to 30 minutes of aerobic exercise at your target heart rate. People can also increase fitness by gradually trying to exercise for longer periods at a faster pace. Experts say that three to five sessions of such exercise per week are the single most important thing you can do to ensure good health. (See also FITNESS; FITNESS TRAINING; RUNNING; SPORTS AND FITNESS; HEART, 1.)

HEALTHY CHOICES

▶ HUNGER

Hunger is the unpleasant sensation of needing to eat. It is the body's way of saying it is in need of fuel in the form of food.

Hunger should not be confused with APPETITE, which is a learned response to food and eating. Hunger has a purely physiological basis, although the exact mechanisms by which it is triggered are not well understood. Several theories have been suggested to explain how the body makes its need for fuel known to the brain. They range from the emptiness of the stomach, to low levels of GLUCOSE or fat stores, to changes in hormone and opiate levels in response to food (or the lack of it).

However the message is communicated (and it probably involves more than one signal), it is clear that the need for food is sensed in the section of the brain called the *hypothalamus*. The hypothalamus receives and processes many chemical messages received from throughout the body and issues a variety of appropriate "orders" in response. One of these is the order to eat, which the body senses as a physical need for food—in other words, hunger.

In a similar way, the hypothalamus receives the message that the body has received enough fuel. It triggers the order to stop eating by producing the physiological sensation of fullness, or *satiety*. Simply put, hunger and satiety are sensations produced by the brain to act as "on" and "off" switches in regard to eating. (See also BODY METABOLISM; ENERGY, FOOD; HYPOTHALAMUS, **1.**)

▶ IRON

Iron is an essential MINERAL that plays a vital part in a variety of complex body processes. Although it is needed only in very small amounts, iron is one of the body's most important nutrients. It helps form *hemoglobin*, the oxygen-carrying component in red blood cells, and *myoglobin*, the oxygen-carrying component in muscle cells. Roughly 80 percent of the body's iron is contained in the hemoglobin in the blood. Iron is necessary for the manufacture of some of the body's most fundamental substances, including amino acids, hormones, and enzymes. The body normally obtains the iron it needs from foods. Liver, eggs, cereals, and leafy green vegetables are especially rich in iron.

Iron Deficiency   An inadequate diet is the most common cause of iron deficiency. Any significant loss of blood can also produce a temporary

Sampling of Foods Rich in Iron.
The recommended dietary allowance for iron is 10 mg per day for men and women past childbearing age and 18 mg for women of childbearing age. Foods rich in this mineral include meats, fish, poultry, spinach, beans, and peas.

deficiency. Although menstruating women lose only small amounts of blood, they require more iron in their diet than men do.

Even slightly depressed levels of iron in the body can produce symptoms that include lowered energy levels and irritability. Greater deficiencies result in a decrease in the amount of hemoglobin in red blood cells, a condition known as *anemia*. Without enough hemoglobin, the blood cannot carry enough oxygen to the body's cells to support normal energy production. The resulting symptoms are fatigue, weakness, headaches, and reduced resistance to disease.

Iron deficiency occasionally results from the inadequate absorption of iron by the body. This can result from drinking too much tea or coffee with meals; both interfere with the absorption of iron. Increasing the intake of VITAMIN C helps the body to absorb iron more efficiently.

Iron deficiency is a significant health problem in the United States and even more so in developed countries where diets tend to be inadequate. In the developed countries, from 10 to 20 percent of the population (mostly women) is estimated to have iron-deficiency anemia. The condition is treated by increasing the consumption of iron-rich foods and by taking iron supplements, often in conjunction with VITAMINS. (See also ANEMIA, **3**.)

▶ JUNK FOOD

Junk food is any food that is high in CALORIES and provides few nutrients. Many SNACK FOODS and FAST FOODS, such as french fries, potato chips, soft drinks, candy, cake, and cookies, are junk foods. Junk foods are not harmful when they are eaten occasionally. They become a problem when they make up a large part of a person's diet.

Junk food is also called empty-calorie food because it has few NUTRIENTS. It is usually high in FATS, SUGAR, and SALT. Although the body needs these nutrients in limited amounts, most Americans eat far more of them

Junk Food.   *Small amounts of junk food are not harmful. However, most Americans eat more junk food than they should.*

than is required. When people fill up on junk food instead of more nutritious food, they do not get the VITAMINS, MINERALS, and other nutrients their bodies need.

RISK FACTORS
▶ ▶ ▶ ▶ ▶ ▶

In addition, most junk foods are high in calories. People who frequently eat junk food may gain unwanted weight. Excess body weight contributes to many diseases, including heart disease, diabetes, hypertension (high blood pressure), and stroke. A high-fat diet also contributes to colon cancer, heart disease, and gallbladder disease.

You can determine which foods are junk foods by reading labels on food packages before you purchase them. Look at the list of ingredients. If fat, sugar, or salt is listed first or second, it is a main ingredient.

HEALTHY CHOICES
▪▪▪▪▪▪▪▪▪▪▪▪

In fast-food restaurants, ask to see nutritional information. When nutritional information is not available, try to avoid fried foods, heavily salted foods, sweet foods, and foods with heavy, creamy, or oily sauces or dressings. (See also FATS, OILS, AND SWEETS GROUP; FOOD LABELING; RECOMMENDED DIETARY ALLOWANCE.)

▶ **LIFESTYLE**

Lifestyle refers to the way a person lives. It includes a person's day-to-day attitudes, habits, and behavior. Lifestyle has a major influence on health.

How Lifestyle Affects Health   People choose their lifestyle. Early in life, people develop certain behaviors that make them happy. They adopt attitudes and habits that reinforce those behaviors. As a result, they establish behavior patterns. Those patterns involve decisions and trade-offs about work, social life, relationships, and many more elements of daily life that affect health.

Behavior patterns and attitudes can have a positive or a harmful effect on health. For example, people who eat a high-fat diet are increasing their risk for developing a number of serious diseases including cancer and heart disease. On the other hand, people who eat a low-fat diet that

Lifestyle.   *A healthful lifestyle is one in which people get regular aerobic exercise, eat and drink in moderation, eat a balanced diet, and do not smoke.*

follows the RECOMMENDED DIETARY ALLOWANCES are reducing their risk for developing the same diseases.

HEALTHY CHOICES

In general, decisions about DIETS and EXERCISE have a major impact on health. Eating a balanced diet and exercising regularly not only will give you more stamina and help you feel good about yourself now but also will help you to avoid many diseases in the future. Several other habits also are essential to promoting health and reducing risk. They include not smoking, drinking only in moderation, eating in proportion to exercise habits, maintaining recommended weight, wearing seat belts in cars and helmets while cycling, and getting enough REST.

RISK FACTORS

Attitudes also affect health, although in ways that are not as well understood. *Stress,* for example, may be generally damaging to health and increase the risk of a number of unhealthy medical conditions. (See also ATTITUDES, 5; STRESS, 5.)

Making Healthful Choices You cannot control every aspect of your health, but you can make decisions about your lifestyle that have a positive effect on your health and well-being. Finding the proper balance of diet, exercise, family, social life, work, and other factors that is right for you is critical. If you establish a healthful lifestyle of moderation early in life, you are more likely to follow it as you grow older.

No two people will make the same lifestyle choices. The important thing is establishing behaviors and attitudes that are fulfilling and promote happiness. (See also RISK FACTORS.)

LIPOSUCTION

Liposuction is a surgical procedure that removes unwanted fat from the body. It is usually performed on people who have large deposits of fat in certain body areas, such as the hips or thighs, that do not respond to DIETS and EXERCISE.

The Procedure A small incision is made in the skin of the area to be treated. A metal straw is then inserted under the skin, and the fat is dislodged and drawn out of the body by a suction machine. The average procedure lasts 1 to 2 hours and removes between 1 and 2 pounds (about 0.5 to 0.9 kg) of fat. It is usually performed under general anesthesia. If the area to be suctioned is small (such as the chin), the procedure may be shorter (less than 30 minutes), and local anesthesia may be used.

Effectiveness and Risk Factors Liposuction is not effective in people who are significantly OVERWEIGHT. In addition, it is not a cure for being overweight. Although liposuction permanently removes fat cells from the body, any fat cells that remain in the treated area will grow larger if the person gains weight. This is because the procedure will not change the underlying factors that lead to weight gain .

Like all surgery, liposuction does have risks. The treated area may become permanently discolored and develop dents. Temporary effects include bruising, swelling, or numbness. Blood clots, infections, and shock can also occur after liposuction. (See also BODY COMPOSITION; PLASTIC SURGERY, 3.)

▶ MACROBIOTIC DIET

A macrobiotic diet is a VEGETARIAN DIET that is based on Oriental philosophy. In this philosophy, foods are either yin (female) or yang (male). Followers of macrobiotic diets believe that eating a diet that balances yin and yang foods will help them enjoy a long, healthy life.

A macrobiotic diet consists entirely of vegetables, fruits, and grains, including nuts, seeds, seaweed, soybean products, and herbal teas. Food is classified as either yin or yang according to its taste, color, texture, and appearance and according to where it is grown. Some macrobiotic diets further restrict the foods that can be eaten. The *Zen macrobiotic diet,* for example, consists only of brown rice and teas and is said to purify the body by cleansing it of harmful *toxins.*

Like all vegetarian diets, macrobiotic diets can be deficient in PROTEIN and certain VITAMINS and MINERALS unless a wide variety of foods is consumed. People on the Zen macrobiotic diet are especially susceptible to health problems associated with a lack of CALCIUM, protein, and vitamins, particularly VITAMIN C. For example, followers of the Zen diet have been known to develop *scurvy,* a disease caused by vitamin C deficiency.

Some people believe that a macrobiotic diet can cure *cancer* by cleansing the body of toxins. There is no scientific evidence that it does so. In fact, the evidence seems to show that it can be harmful. Cancer patients who choose to follow a macrobiotic diet instead of traditional medical treatments risk weight loss and MALNUTRITION and lose any possible benefits available from proven therapies. (See also DIETS; FAD DIETS.)

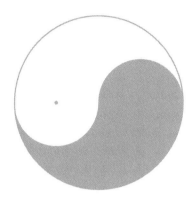

Yin-Yang Symbol. *A macrobiotic diet is part of the Oriental philosophy involving yin and yang.*

▶ MALNUTRITION

Malnutrition is an unhealthy condition caused by a lack of NUTRIENTS in the body. Worldwide, it is a major health problem responsible for millions of deaths annually, especially of children. In the United States, malnutrition is much less common. It primarily affects the poor. It also affects those on DIETS that do not provide the body with enough of the right kinds of nutrients. Malnutrition may also result from diseases that prevent the body from absorbing or using nutrients properly.

RISK FACTORS
▶ ▶ ▶ ▶ ▶ ▶

Symptoms of malnutrition vary depending on the nutrient or nutrients missing from the diet or the disease that causes it. In general, however, malnourished people experience diarrhea, weakness, weight loss, stunted growth, and susceptibility to infection. Children who are malnourished are often anemic and small for their age, and they often have poor dental health.

Malnutrition Caused by Deficiencies in the Diet   Dietary deficiencies may result when people have poor eating habits or food preferences, or when certain foods containing essential vitamins and minerals are unavailable. Common deficiencies include PROTEINS, CALORIES, VITAMINS, and MINERALS. These deficiencies often overlap.

When a person's diet lacks adequate amounts of protein and calories, the result is a disease called *kwashiorkor* (kwash ee OR kur). Symptoms include a swollen face and stomach; patchy, flaking skin; weakness; stunted growth; and low resistance to sickness. Kwashiorkor also damages vital organs such as the intestines, liver, and pancreas. This disease

Malnutrition. *In many less developed parts of the world, malnutrition occurs as a result of social or economic conditions such as floods, drought, poverty, war, disease, and ignorance.*

commonly affects children in poor countries after they stop getting nourishment from their mother's BREAST MILK.

A deficiency of calories and nutrients leads to *marasmus*, another disease that is common in poor countries. A person with marasmus is very thin, with little or no fat under the skin. All muscles, including the heart, are wasted. This disease most commonly affects children from 6 to 18 months of age. Since the brain grows rapidly at that time, marasmus often impairs brain development and learning ability.

A person who lacks adequate amounts of proteins and calories has *protein-calorie malnutrition*. This disease is the most common form of malnutrition among children in the developing world. Its primary symptom is stunted growth.

Vitamin or mineral deficiencies may also cause malnutrition. The diseases that result vary depending on the missing nutrient. For example, anemia is caused by a lack of iron or copper in the blood. (See also ANEMIA, **3**.)

Malnutrition Caused by Disease   Conditions and diseases that affect the body's ability to absorb or use the nutrients in food may cause malnutrition. Some of these conditions such as tumors, infections, or inflammation affect the intestines. Lack of absorption may occur as a result of intolerance to lactose (a sugar in milk) or to a protein in wheat or rye flours or as a result of a variety of rare acquired or inherited defects. The symptoms of intestinal conditions usually include abdominal discomfort and weight loss.

RISK FACTORS
▶ ▶ ▶ ▶ ▶ ▶

Disturbances of the endocrine system or liver can also affect the body's use of nutrients. Diabetes mellitus is an example of an endocrine disease that can cause nutritional wasting. Finally, people with certain psychological disorders, including anorexia nervosa, may decrease their food intake to levels that cause malnutrition. (See also EATING DISORDERS.)

RISK FACTORS
▶ ▶ ▶ ▶ ▶ ▶

Groups Affected by Malnutrition   The group most seriously affected by malnutrition is children. The United Nations reports that 10 million children under the age of 5 are severely malnourished. Young children are particularly susceptible because they need more nutrients to fuel their growth and development. Poverty and lack of food, especially in developing countries, often prevent children from getting the nutrients they need. Parental neglect and lack of nutritional knowledge often add to the problem.

The elderly are also prone to malnutrition. This may be the result of poverty or a lack of food. It may also be a function of disability, social isolation, or loneliness, all of which tend to afflict the elderly. People who are lonely, for example, may have a depressed APPETITE and may lack the motivation to shop for food and prepare and eat healthy meals.

Alcoholics are also affected by malnutrition. Alcohol depresses the appetite so that many heavy drinkers eat poorly if at all. Even heavy drinkers who eat well may be malnourished because alcohol prevents the absorption of nutrients, changes BODY METABOLISM, and increases the rate of excretion of many nutrients. (See also ALCOHOLISM, 7.)

Preventing Malnutrition   Global malnutrition is a complex political and economic problem closely associated with poverty. It requires solutions that provide more effective food production and distribution systems, especially in developing countries. In the United States, social programs and agencies help ensure that many people in high-risk groups receive adequate nutrition. Still, many in need slip through these "safety nets" and suffer the damaging health effects of malnutrition. (See also NUTRITION; UNDERWEIGHT.)

▶ MEATS, EGGS, AND LEGUMES GROUP   The meats, eggs, and legumes food group is a class of foods that includes beef, pork, poultry, fish, shellfish, eggs, nuts, beans, and peas. All these foods are high in PROTEIN, which is an essential NUTRIENT for building new body cells. Many foods in this group are also important sources of VITAMINS and MINERALS. Some, however, are high in FATS and CHOLESTEROL, which have been linked to heart disease.

Foods in This Group   *Meat* is the muscle or flesh of cattle (beef and veal), sheep (lamb), and pigs (pork, ham, and bacon). Meat is sold in cuts, such as shoulder or loin, that indicate the part of the animal's body from which the cut was taken. *Organ meats*, such as heart, liver, and kidney, are especially rich in certain vitamins and minerals. *Processed meats*, including sausage, hot dogs, and luncheon meats, have been smoked or seasoned.

Poultry includes chickens, turkeys, ducks, geese, and game birds. Poultry is high in protein, rich in several important vitamins and minerals, and substantially lower in fat than meat. In addition to eating poultry, most Americans eat chicken *eggs*. Eggs are a good protein substitute for meat, but egg yolks contain high amounts of fat and cholesterol.

Fish, another food in this group, may come from salt water (the ocean) or fresh water (lakes, rivers, and streams). Examples of saltwater fish are cod, halibut, tuna, and swordfish. Freshwater fish includes trout

High-Protein Foods. *Foods in this group are high in protein as well as rich in many important vitamins and minerals.*

and bass. Examples of *shellfish* are shrimp, lobster, crab, and clams. Like poultry, fish (but not shellfish) is generally lower in fat and cholesterol than is meat.

Legumes are seeds that grow in a pod. They include *nuts* and *seeds*, which are plant kernels that usually come enclosed in a shell. Almonds, peanuts, pine nuts, and pumpkin seeds are examples of nuts and seeds. *Peas* and *beans*, including kidney beans, chick peas, green peas, peanuts, and soybeans, are also legumes. As a class, legumes are lower in fat than are the other foods in this group. In addition, legumes—because they are plants—have no cholesterol.

Nutrition from Meats, Eggs, and Legumes Meats, poultry, eggs, and most fish provide complete proteins, whereas most nuts and legumes supply incomplete proteins. *Complete proteins* include all the *essential amino acids*, the components the body needs to build cells. *Incomplete proteins* lack one or more of these essential amino acids. Among plant foods, only soybeans, dried yeast, and wheat germ have complete proteins. However, people can easily obtain complete proteins by combining nuts or legumes with grains or meats. Together these *complementary proteins* supply all the essential amino acids. For example, the beans and meat in chili con carne or the legumes and grains in a peanut butter sandwich complement each other to provide complete proteins.

Excess protein cannot be stored in the body, and protein is therefore needed as part of the daily diet. Protein deficiency, although a major nutritional problem in some parts of the world, is rare in the United States. Nearly all Americans get as much or more protein than their bodies need for good nutrition.

In addition to protein, foods in the meats, eggs, and legumes group also provide significant amounts of VITAMIN A, VITAMIN B COMPLEX, and the minerals IRON, zinc, and phosphorus. Because exact nutrient content varies from one food to another, choosing a wide variety of foods from this group is the best way to ensure adequate amounts of these important nutrients.

Although fat is an important nutrient, most Americans eat too much of it. Overconsumption of fat, especially the saturated fat typical in animal fats, can cause a person to become OVERWEIGHT and may lead to heart disease and other health problems. Nutritionists advise Americans to cut down on fat- and cholesterol-rich foods, particularly meat, and to eat more poultry, fish, grains, and fruits and vegetables. Cooking methods also make a difference. When preparing poultry, for example, you should remove the skin, which contains a lot of fat. Avoid deep-frying foods or cooking them in large amounts of fat or oil. Lean cuts of meat should be chosen whenever possible.

HEALTHY CHOICES

Daily Servings of Meats, Eggs, and Legumes The FOUR FOOD GROUPS SYSTEM and the FIVE FOOD GROUPS SYSTEM recommend that people eat two servings of meats, eggs, and legumes per day. The FOOD PYRAMID SYSTEM suggests two to three servings per day. In general, you should try to choose foods from this group that are low in fat and cholesterol. (See also BREADS AND CEREALS GROUP; DIETARY GUIDELINES; EXCHANGE SYSTEM; FATS, OILS, AND SWEETS GROUP; FOOD GROUP SYSTEMS; FRUITS AND VEGETABLES GROUP; MILK AND MILK PRODUCTS GROUP; HEART DISEASE, **3**.)

▶ MILK AND MILK PRODUCTS GROUP

The milk and milk products group, sometimes called the dairy products group, is a class of foods that have milk as their main ingredient. Foods in this group include cheese, yogurt, and ice cream, as well as milk. In the United States, most milk comes from cows; in many other countries, however, people also use the milk of goats, camels, sheep, and llamas. Milk and milk products are the chief source of calcium in the American diet, but this food group also provides many other NUTRIENTS.

Nutrition from Milk and Milk Products Milk has been called the most nearly perfect food because it contains so many of the nutrients that the human body needs to live and grow. All milk products are rich in CALCIUM, a mineral essential for strong bones and teeth. Milk also contains a large amount of WATER, as well as CARBOHYDRATES, PROTEINS, and FATS.

Milk also contains a variety of essential VITAMINS and MINERALS. It is a good source of vitamins A, E, and K, and riboflavin, a B vitamin. In the United States, vitamin D is added to milk because it helps the body use calcium. Besides calcium, milk contains minerals such as phosphorus, potassium, and SODIUM.

Because milk comes from animals, it is high in saturated fat and CHOLESTEROL, which have been linked to heart disease. Therefore, nutritionists recommend that people switch from whole milk to low-fat or skim milk and choose milk products that have reduced fat.

HEALTHY CHOICES

Types of Milk and Milk Products Milk can be found in several forms. *Whole milk* is that from which no fat has been removed. *Low-fat milk* contains only 1 or 2 percent fat, and *skim milk* is milk from which nearly all the fat has been removed. These products are usually *pasteurized* (heated and cooled to kill bacteria) and *homogenized* (blended to mix the

Milk and Milk Products Group. *The foods in this group are good sources of calcium.*

fats into the liquid). Evaporated and condensed milk, from which much of the water has been removed, are available in cans. *Nonfat dry milk,* or powdered milk, is milk from which all liquid has been removed. Water is added to the powder to produce milk in liquid form.

The *butterfat* or *cream* in milk is used to make butter and ice cream. It is also sold separately as cream or half-and-half, a mixture of milk and cream. Butter is pasteurized cream that is stirred or churned until the fat forms into a solid. (Because of its high fat content, butter is usually considered part of the FATS, OILS, AND SWEETS GROUP.) Ice cream and ice milk are frozen products made from cream or milk, sugar, and flavorings.

Yogurt, sour cream, and buttermilk are called *cultured milk products* because they are produced by adding cultures of harmless bacteria to milk or cream. This gives them a thicker texture and a tangy taste. Special ingredients are also added to milk to make cheese. The ingredients cause the milk to separate into solid and liquid parts. The solids are then pressed into molds and aged to create cheese. There are more than 400 kinds of cheese.

People who are *lactose intolerant* have trouble digesting milk. They are missing or deficient in an enzyme (a chemical protein) necessary to break down *lactose* (milk sugar), the carbohydrate component of milk. An enzyme supplement is available to enable people who are lactose intolerant to drink milk. Many people who are lactose intolerant also find they can eat cultured milk products and cheeses without experiencing problems.

Daily Servings of Milk and Milk Products Both the FOUR FOOD GROUPS SYSTEM and the FIVE FOOD GROUPS SYSTEM suggest varying numbers of servings from this group depending on an individual's age. Teenagers and young adults need four servings each day, children up to the age of 10 need three servings, and adults need only two servings. (See also BREADS AND CEREALS GROUP; DIETARY GUIDELINES; EXCHANGE SYSTEM; FOOD GROUP SYSTEMS; FOOD PYRAMID SYSTEM; FRUITS AND VEGETABLES GROUP; MEATS, EGGS, AND LEGUMES GROUP; HEART DISEASE, **3.**)

HEALTHY CHOICES
●●●●●●●●●●●●●

MINERALS

Minerals are inorganic substances in food that play a vital part in BODY METABOLISM—the complex life processes that occur within the body. There are many different minerals, each performing various responsibilities. Some help in the function of muscles, the transmission of nerve impulses, or the regulation of fluid and chemical levels in the body. Others are needed to form bones, teeth, and tissues or to regulate body temperature. Most of the foods we eat contain at least some minerals.

There are more than 60 minerals, which are classified into two groups according to the quantities found in the body. *Macrominerals* are found in large quantities. This group of minerals includes CALCIUM, POTASSIUM, SODIUM, phosphorus, magnesium, and chloride (chlorine). *Microminerals,* also called *trace minerals,* are found in smaller amounts. IRON, iodine, sulphur, zinc, copper, manganese, fluoride (fluorine), chromium, selenium, and molybdenum are among the microminerals.

Mineral deficiencies in the United States are rare because most people get the amounts they need by eating a well-balanced diet. In addition, the body holds reserves of most minerals, releasing them as they are needed. Supplements of some minerals—for example, iron and calcium—are sometimes necessary, however, but should be taken only with a doctor's advice (see chart: Recommended Dietary Allowances of Minerals).

RISK FACTORS
▶ ▶ ▶ ▶ ▶ ▶

Calcium   Calcium is essential in building healthy bones and teeth. Deficiencies of calcium are relatively common and can contribute to *osteoporosis*, a disease characterized by a dangerous and sometimes crippling loss of bone mass.

Potassium   Potassium is essential to cell metabolism, the transmission of nerve impulses, and the functioning of muscles. Potassium also operates in conjunction with sodium to control blood pressure.

Sodium   Sodium performs many of the same roles as potassium, including the regulation of blood pressure. Too much sodium in the diet (found in table salt, among other forms) is associated with *hypertension* (high blood pressure).

Phosphorus   Most of the phosphorus in the body combines with calcium and forms calcium phosphate, which helps build and maintain bones and teeth. Phosphorus plays a variety of other roles in cellular metabolism, including helping with the transfer of energy and nutrients. Because phosphorus occurs in almost all foods, deficiencies are rare.

Magnesium   Magnesium performs numerous functions. It helps cells use energy, break down *proteins* and *carbohydrates*, transmit nerve impulses, and regulate body temperature. Magnesium deficiencies can be caused by persistent vomiting or diarrhea, kidney disease, diabetes, alcoholism, and the use of certain medications. Raw leafy green vegetables, nuts, whole-grain products, and seafood are all excellent sources of magnesium.

HEALTHY CHOICES
▪●●●●●●●●●●●▪

Chloride   Chloride performs several important functions. It helps maintain the acid-base balance in the digestive fluids in the stomach as well as in other body fluids. Chloride also helps the blood carry carbon dioxide

RECOMMENDED DIETARY ALLOWANCES OF MINERALS

Category (age, sex, or condition)	Calcium (mg)	Phosphorus (mg)	Magnesium (mg)	Iron (mg)	Zinc (mg)	Iodine (mcg)	Selenium (mcg)	Copper* (mg)	Manganese* (mg)	Fluoride* (mg)	Chromium* (mcg)	Molybdenum* (mcg)
Infants												
0–½	400	300	40	6	5	40	10	0.4–0.6	0.3–0.6	0.1–0.5	10–40	15–30
½–1	600	500	60	10	5	50	15	0.6–0.7	0.6–1.0	0.2–1.0	20–60	20–40
Children												
1–3	800	800	80	10	10	70	20	0.7–1.0	1.0–1.5	0.5–1.5	20–80	25–50
4–6	800	800	120	10	10	90	20	1.0–1.5	1.5–2.0	1.0–2.5	30–120	30–75
7–10	800	800	170	10	10	120	30	1.0–2.0	2.0–3.0	1.5–2.5	50–200	50–150
Males												
11–14	1,200	1,200	270	12	15	150	40	1.5–2.5	2.0–5.0	1.5–2.5	50–200	75–250
15–18	1,200	1,200	400	12	15	150	50	1.5–2.5	2.0–5.0	1.5–2.5	50–200	75–250
19–24	1,200	1,200	350	10	15	150	70	1.5–3.0	2.0–5.0	1.5–4.0	50–200	75–250
25–50	800	800	350	10	15	150	70	1.5–3.0	2.0–5.0	1.5–4.0	50–200	75–250
51+	800	800	350	10	15	150	70	1.5–3.0	2.0–5.0	1.5–4.0	50–200	75–250
Females												
11–14	1,200	1,200	280	15	12	150	45	1.5–2.5	2.0–5.0	1.5–2.5	50–200	75–250
15–18	1,200	1,200	300	15	12	150	50	1.5–2.5	2.0–5.0	1.5–2.5	50–200	75–250
19–24	1,200	1,200	280	15	12	150	55	1.5–3.0	2.0–5.0	1.5–4.0	50–200	75–250
25–50	800	800	280	15	12	150	55	1.5–3.0	2.0–5.0	1.5–4.0	50–200	75–250
51+	800	800	280	10	12	150	55	1.5–3.0	2.0–5.0	1.5–4.0	50–200	75–250
Pregnant females	1,200	1,200	300	30	15	175	65	1.5–3.0	2.0–5.0	1.5–4.0	50–200	75–250
Lactating females												
1st 6 months	1,200	1,200	355	15	19	200	75	1.5–3.0	2.0–5.0	1.5–4.0	50–200	75–250
2nd 6 months	1,200	1,200	340	15	16	200	75	1.5–3.0	2.0–5.0	1.5–4.0	50–200	75–250

*Information for these minerals is provided as estimated safe and adequate daily intakes, rather than as recommended allowances.

Adapted with permission from *Recommended Dietary Allowances, 10th edition.* Copyright 1989 by the National Academy of Sciences. Published by the National Academy Press, Washington, D.C.

(a waste product) to the lungs. Chloride deficiencies are rare. Most people get adequate amounts from table salt (sodium chloride).

Iron Needed only in small amounts, iron performs a variety of important functions within the body. Most significantly, it is necessary for the formation of red blood cells, which transport essential oxygen throughout the body. A deficiency of iron can result in *anemia,* a blood disorder that results in fatigue, weakness, and impaired mental abilities.

RISK FACTORS
▶ ▶ ▶ ▶ ▶ ▶

Iodine Iodine occurs in the body in very small amounts. However, it plays a vital role in the activities of the *thyroid hormones,* which are involved in reproduction, growth, nerve and muscle function, and the production of new blood cells. Low levels of iodine can result in an enlarged thyroid gland, a condition known as *goiter.* Too much iodine can also cause a condition resembling goiter. Iodine is normally added to table salt, which enables the average American to get enough in a normal diet.

Sulphur Sulphur ensures that *proteins* (an essential part of every cell) form and maintain a shape that is appropriate to the function they serve. Large concentrations of sulphur are found in rigid tissues such as the skin, hair, and nails. Sulphur deficiencies are unknown.

Zinc Zinc performs a variety of functions in the muscles, skin, bones, eyes, liver, kidneys, and male reproductive organs. It helps to activate more than 70 different *enzymes* (substances that trigger reactions), increase the infection-fighting ability of white blood cells, and promote the manufacture of sperm in men. It also plays an important part in growth and development. Zinc deficiencies can occur and can inhibit growth and sexual maturation. Foods such as shellfish, meat, and whole-grain breads can prevent a zinc deficiency.

HEALTHY CHOICES

Copper The micromineral copper interacts with iron to help prevent anemia. In addition, copper is involved in creating hair pigment, the sheaths surrounding nerve fibers, and elastin and collagen, elements of connective tissue. Copper deficiency is rare but can result from an inability to absorb it properly. Liver, shellfish, nuts, and mushrooms are among the many rich sources of copper.

Manganese Among its many important functions, manganese helps create fatty acids and cholesterol and metabolize carbohydrates. It is also necessary for normal bone and connective-tissue development. Deficiency of manganese is unknown, but too much can cause serious problems such as weakness, muscle rigidity, and mental abnormalities. Manganese toxicity usually does not result from high dietary intake but from industrial contamination. Nuts, whole-grain cereals, dried beans, and tea are all rich in manganese.

Fluoride Fluoride is necessary for strong bones and teeth. It helps protect children's teeth from decay and may delay the progress of osteoporosis in adults. Fluoridated water, fish, tea, and fluoridated toothpastes are the usual sources of fluoride.

HEALTHY CHOICES

Chromium The body needs chromium in order to effectively use the sugar glucose, the primary food of cells. A deficiency of chromium in adults has been associated with diabetes. In children, it has been linked to slowed growth. Vegetables, whole grains, fruits, and cheese are high in chromium.

Selenium The micromineral selenium helps protect cells against damage from oxygen-derived compounds. A selenium deficiency can cause heart problems and may be linked to certain types of cancer. Foods grown in regions with selenium-poor soil may be low in this mineral. Too much selenium is also dangerous and can cause loss of hair and nails, damage to skin and teeth, and problems with the nervous system.

Molybdenum Molybdenum helps produce uric acid and helps the body make use of iron stored in the liver. It may also help prevent tooth decay. Deficiencies of molybdenum are unknown. Too much of this mineral can result in goutlike symptoms such as pain and swelling in joints. Peas, beans, and meat are the best sources of this trace mineral. (See also RECOMMENDED DIETARY ALLOWANCE; NUTRIENTS; VITAMINS.)

MONOSODIUM GLUTAMATE

Monosodium glutamate, or *MSG,* is a SALT that forms when SODIUM is combined with glutamic acid, an *amino acid* found in all foods containing protein. It is widely used in food processing and preparation to enhance the natural flavor of meats, poultry, seafood, soups, and vegetables.

81. Bean Curd Hunan Style (with or without porl

○ 82. Broccoli in Garlic Sauce (with or without pc

83. Sauteed Broccoli. . . . .

84. Eggplant with Brown Sauce. . . . .

85. Buddhist Delight (mixed Vegetables). . . . . .

86. Sauteed Snow Peas & Water Chestnuts. . . . .

* **Our dishes are available without MSG**

MSG Content in Chinese Dishes. *Until recently, monosodium glutamate was routinely added to virtually all foods in Chinese restaurants, but now many dishes can be prepared without this food additive.*

 RISK FACTORS ▶ ▶ ▶ ▶ ▶ ▶

MSG has been linked to a condition known as *Chinese restaurant syndrome.* Although recent studies have revealed that MSG has no specific toxic effects when consumed in normal quantities, people sensitive to this substance may experience symptoms including dizziness, chest pain, headache, and a burning or tingling in the arms and neck shortly after eating foods containing high levels of monosodium glutamate. The symptoms disappear after a short period of time. (See also FOOD ADDITIVES.)

MSG

see MONOSODIUM GLUTAMATE

NATURAL FOOD

see ORGANIC FOOD

NUTRIENTS

Nutrients are substances in food that are essential for good health. They build, maintain, and repair body tissues; regulate body processes; and provide fuel for energy. There are five essential nutrients of two basic types. The *macronutrients,* so called because they are required in large quantities, are carbohydrates, fats, and proteins. Minerals and vitamins, on the other hand, are needed only in very small amounts and are therefore classified as *micronutrients.* It is important to eat a varied and balanced diet because nutrients work together to maintain health (see chart: Basic Nutrients in Select Foods).

BASIC NUTRIENTS IN SELECT FOODS

| Food | Macronutrients | | | Vitamins | | | Minerals | | |
	Fat (g)	Protein (g)	Carbo-hydrates (g)	Vitamin A (retinol equivalents)	Thiamine (mg)	Vitamin C (mg)	Calcium (mg)	Iron (mg)	Sodium (mg)
Apple (1 large)	1	—	32	11	0.04	12	15	0.4	—
Orange (1 medium)	—	1	15	27	0.11	70	52	0.1	—
Bagel	2	7	38	0	0.26	0	29	1.8	245
Cracked-wheat bread (1 slice)	1	2	12	—	0.10	—	16	0.7	106
Kellogg's Special K (1⅓ cup)	—	6	21	375*	0.37*	15*	8	4.5*	265
Asparagus cuts and tips, fresh, cooked (1 cup)	1	5	8	149	0.18	49	43	1.2	7
Carrot, raw (1 medium)	—	1	7	2,025	0.07	7	19	0.4	25
Whole milk (1 cup)	8	8	11	76	0.09	2	291	0.1	120
Skim milk (1 cup)	—	8	12	149	0.09	2	302	0.1	126
Tuna, in oil (3 oz)	7	24	0	20	0.04	0	7	1.6	303
Ground beef, lean (3 oz)	16	21	0	—	0.04	0	9	1.8	65
Bologna (1 slice)	16	7	2	0	0.10	—	7	0.9	581
Chicken breast, fried (5.6 oz)	18	35	13	28	0.16	0	28	1.8	385

*Nutrient added.

Source: U.S. Department of Agriculture.

Macronutrients CARBOHYDRATES provide energy in two basic forms, STARCH and SUGAR. A third type of carbohydrate, FIBER, is undigestible but helps the body eliminate solid waste by providing bulk (or roughage). Carbohydrates are found in nonanimal foods, especially grains, vegetables, and fruits. FATS are the body's source of reserve energy. They also insulate the body against excessive heat loss and help store and use vitamins. Foods containing fats include butter, meat, salad dressings, cheese, and milk. PROTEINS build and maintain body tissues. Animal products (meat, fish, milk, eggs) are high-protein foods. Vegetables, fruits, and grains also contain protein, but these proteins are incomplete.

Micronutrients MINERALS help maintain vital body processes, including the function of muscles, the manufacture of red blood cells, the transmission of nerve impulses, and the formation and maintenance of bones and teeth. The essential minerals are calcium, iron, sodium, iodide, phosphorus, potassium, and zinc. VITAMINS, found in many kinds of foods, help regulate numerous bodily processes.

NUTRITION

Nutrition is the relation of food to human health. Nutrition also refers to the scientific study of food NUTRIENTS and the processes through which they nourish the human body.

Good Nutrition Versus Poor Nutrition Good nutrition is vital to human health and well-being. A varied, well-balanced diet appropriate in amount is the basic source of good nutrition.

On the other hand, too little food, especially low-nutrient food, results in MALNUTRITION, which contributes to many diseases and disorders. Too much food and too little exercise cause OBESITY and its associated medical problems. Imbalances in the diet are also examples of poor nutrition. For example, heart disease and some types of cancer may result when people eat too much fat. Too much salt in the diet can aggravate hypertension (high blood pressure) in susceptible individuals. People who eat large amounts of sugar may have inadequate VITAMIN and MINERAL intake, which can lead to a variety of health problems in addition to tooth decay.

The Science of Nutrition Nutrition is a relatively young science. It was not recognized as a separate area of study until 1934 but has grown

Good Nutrition. *Good nutrition starts with a well-balanced diet of healthful foods.*

in importance since that time. Much has been learned about the links between diet and health. For example, 40 years ago many people had not heard of CHOLESTEROL. Now most people know that a diet high in saturated fat and cholesterol may result in blocked arteries and contribute to heart disease.

The science of nutrition covers a broad range of issues and concerns. Nutritional scientists investigate how the essential nutrients affect growth, disease, and metabolism. *Nutritionists* address questions about what foods people should eat and how changes in diet affect people. They study how foods are digested, absorbed, and used by the human body. (See also BODY METABOLISM.)

Nutritionists also apply nutritional principles directly in the treatment of disease. *Nutritional therapy* adjusts diet to help heal or control diseases. For instance, many people with diabetes mellitus are able to control their disease without medication by following a sugar-free diet. In addition, a low-protein diet can slow the progression of chronic liver failure, and vitamin therapy is useful in treating certain kinds of cancer.

Dietetics   Dietetics is the science of applying the principles of nutrition to the DIETS of individuals and groups. *Dietitians* are people who are trained to use those principles to plan diets. For example, dietitians develop low-fat diets for people who want to control blood cholesterol levels and lose weight and low-salt diets for people with hypertension. They also give people advice on eating out on a diet and how to shop for foods. (See also PHYTOCHEMICALS; CANCER, **3**; DIABETES, **3**; HEART DISEASE, **3**; HYPERTENSION, **3**; NUTRITIONIST, **9**.)

▶ OBESITY

Importance of Exercise. *By combining a regular exercise program with a sensible diet, many individuals can lose weight effectively and remain healthy.*

Obesity is a condition in which an excess amount of body fat causes a person's weight to be more than 20 percent above the maximum weight recommended for his or her height and sex. Obesity is a major health problem in the United States, afflicting roughly 25 percent of the population. Even mild obesity is a health hazard, because it increases the risk of certain diseases and physical problems. (See also OVERWEIGHT.)

Causes of Obesity   The causes of obesity are not completely clear; the tendency to be obese is in part hereditary. Obesity occurs as excess body fat builds up when the number of calories consumed exceeds the number expended. This depends on an individual's BODY METABOLISM, the rate at which energy is used by the body. Some obese people have very slow metabolic rates. Others do not; their obesity may be the result of overeating or of a lack of physical EXERCISE. In many cases, hereditary and behavioral factors work together to cause obesity.

Health Risks   Obesity has many health risks. It can increase the chances of high blood pressure, stroke, diabetes, heart disease, and certain types of cancer, for instance. Extra weight on the back, hips, and knees can strain joints. Losing weight produces substantial health benefits for obese people. It improves general health, increases life expectancy, and often enhances a person's sense of well-being.

Treatment   To lose weight, an obese person should follow a WEIGHT-LOSS STRATEGY. Losing 1 to 2 pounds per week until the goal is reached is considered safe. Regular exercise can help maintain a steady weight loss. FAD DIETS with a very low calorie intake do not produce good long-term results; lost weight is usually regained. Group weight-loss programs can offer information and support. A sensible combination of changes to the diet, new eating habits, and exercise is often the best approach. (See also DIET AIDS; DIET FOOD; DIETS; RISK FACTORS; WEIGHT ASSESSMENT; WEIGHT MANAGEMENT.)

▶ **ORGANIC FOOD**   Organic food is food that is grown and processed without the use of commercial chemicals. When organic food is produced, no *chemical fertilizers, pesticides,* or FOOD ADDITIVES are intentionally used.

Many people believe that organic food is healthier than other food because organic matter, such as manure and compost (rotted leaves and other vegetable materials), is used instead of factory-produced chemicals as fertilizer. Some organic foods do contain fewer such chemicals than do other foods. However, many organic foods contain the same amount and kinds of chemicals as foods grown with chemical fertilizers and pesticides. This may result from organic foods being grown in soils that were previously treated with AGRICULTURAL CHEMICALS. The chemicals remain in the soil for years, affecting crops that are grown there. In addition, if nearby farmers spray their crops with pesticides, wind, rain, and groundwater can carry the chemicals to the fields of organic farmers.

Organic food is not any more or less nutritious than other food, but organic food is usually more expensive. Some of the additional expense comes from labor costs. Because no chemical pesticides or weed killers are used, weeds and insects must be removed by hand.

The quality and appearance of organic food are often inferior to that of other food. Chemical fertilizers convey NUTRIENTS to plants. Plants that are grown with organic fertilizers may not obtain the MINERALS they need. Organically grown fruits and vegetables may also be unattractive because pesticides are not used to keep insects from biting or boring holes in the skins.

On the other hand, proponents of organic food point out that the long-term safety for consumption of many agricultural chemicals is open to question. And, in fact, a few pesticides have been withdrawn from the market after decades of use when proved to be potentially unsafe for consumption. In addition, organic food-production methods are generally thought to be less harmful to the environment, a concern for many consumers.

When consumers buy food, they should carefully compare the cost, appearance, and nutritional value of organic food against that of other food. In addition, they should remember that the term *organic* has no legal meaning and food producers can use that label to mean anything they choose. (See also FOOD SAFETY; FOOD AND DRUG ADMINISTRATION, 7; AGRICULTURAL POLLUTION, 8.)

Organic Food.   *Until the government sets official standards for food labeled "organic," the only way consumers can be sure of what they are buying is to read labels and ask questions.*

▶ OVERWEIGHT

To be overweight is to weigh 10 to 20 percent more than the recommended weight range for your height and sex. Overweight is a problem only if excess weight is in fat, as it is in most overweight people. Being slightly overweight is not a serious problem. A person whose weight is greater than 20 percent above the recommended range is considered obese. OBESITY is a major risk factor for a number of health problems.

A common method for determining overweight and obesity is the *body-mass index* (BMI). The BMI ratio is determined by dividing weight (in kilograms) by height (in meters squared). A BMI of 20 to 25 is generally considered acceptable; significant health risks are associated with an index of 27 or above. Other methods for determining whether a person is overweight include height and weight charts and the waist-to-hip ratio. (See also WEIGHT ASSESSMENT.)

Balanced Diet. *Eating a balanced, low-calorie diet and getting enough exercise is the safest way to lose weight and keep it off.*

Causes Many factors can cause someone to become overweight. The tendency to overweight seems to be hereditary to some degree. Poor eating habits (especially a high-fat diet) and a lack of exercise are major causes of weight gain. A person with a tendency to be overweight can easily gain weight over time if there is an increase in calories consumed or a decrease in calories burned. Whatever the cause, being obese is bad for your health, bringing an increased risk of high blood pressure, diabetes, and heart disease, among other damaging conditions.

RISK FACTORS
▶ ▶ ▶ ▶ ▶ ▶

Treatment Following a sensible WEIGHT-LOSS STRATEGY that combines a reduction in calorie intake with regular, progressive physical exercise will help lose weight. Developing good eating and exercise habits will help keep the weight off once a goal is reached.

HEALTHY CHOICES

▶ PERSPIRATION

Perspiration is loss of water through the skin in the form of sweat. Sweat consists of water, salts, and other substances and is excreted through glands in the skin. Perspiration normally results in a loss of between 12 and 24 ounces (about 350 to 700 mL) of water each day. During

Sweating and Dehydration.
During strenuous activities, heavy perspiration can result in severe water loss, which can be gauged by the decrease in body weight. To avoid dehydration, drink at least 16 ounces (about 500 mL) of water 15 to 30 minutes before exercising and 4 to 8 ounces (100 to 250 mL) every 10 to 20 minutes during exercise. Then drink enough water afterward to replace the water lost in perspiration—about 16 ounces (500 mL) for every pound lost during exercise.

hot weather and vigorous exercise, however, this amount can increase to 1 quart (about 1 L) or more per hour.

When a person exercises, heat is produced. Perspiration helps the body cool itself down. As sweat evaporates from the skin, it takes heat away from the body. This cooling process is most efficient when the air is dry; humidity makes evaporation more difficult. People perspire during cold weather too, especially after exerting themselves significantly.

The Importance of Fluid Replacement Heavy perspiration is a signal that the body is losing WATER quickly. This water must be replaced to help prevent DEHYDRATION, a condition in which the water necessary for the body to function becomes dangerously low. The sense of *thirst* usually prompts the replacement of lost fluids, but during hot weather or intense exercise the body's response may lag far behind its actual need for water. People in these situations must make a conscious effort to drink water before, during, and after exercise (see illustration: Sweating and Dehydration). Although heavy perspiration also results in a loss of salt and some other elements in body fluids, these are easily replaced in the diet. Consuming supplementary salt tablets, once common, is not recommended. (See also BEVERAGES; SPORTS AND HEAT PROBLEMS.)

HEALTHY CHOICES

▶ **PHYTOCHEMICALS**   Phytochemicals are chemical substances found in vegetables, herbs, and other plants. Many phytochemicals are believed to be beneficial to health, protecting human cells from damage, inhibiting processes that lead to cancer and other diseases, and possibly even retarding the aging process. VITAMINS, BETA CAROTENE, and FIBER are all beneficial phytochemicals. But researchers continue to find promising new classes of phytochemicals. Phytochemical research is a relatively new field, however, and more studies are needed to establish a convincing connection between many of these chemical substances and good health.

To date, a number of studies have found potentially beneficial phytochemicals in a range of plants. Garlic, for instance, has sulphur compounds that may help detoxify cancer-causing agents from the environment. Red wine contains a chemical called reservatrol that may reduce heart disease by boosting HDL cholesterol (the "good" cholesterol). Rice oil contains chemicals called phytosterols that are believed to lower blood cholesterol levels. Broccoli and other related vegetables (cauliflower, brussels sprouts, kale) contain sulphuraphane, a compound that may help prevent cancer by helping cell enzymes fight tumors. Citrus fruits contain D-limonene, a chemical that is thought to help prevent breast cancer. And tea, especially green tea, contains high levels of polyphenols, substances that act as *antioxidants* and may help ward off cancer by neutralizing cell-destroying substances called *free radicals*.

The notion of special disease-fighting or -preventing qualities in specific foods is nothing new. Since ancient times, folk medicine has promoted the benefits of certain foods and herbs and developed tonics and treatments from plants. Contemporary research in cellular metabolism is beginning to explain some of their workings. Many foods recently identified as beneficial correlate closely to foods promoted in folk medicine. This has led some researchers to theorize that people's tastes may be shaped to some extent by an innate knowledge of what is good for them.

The U.S. Department of Agriculture's Research Center on Aging is coordinating phytochemical research being conducted at universities around the country, and in 1990 the National Cancer Institute began a 5-year study to examine how chemicals in common foods can fight cancer. Although more research needs to be done before the effects of phytochemicals on health are clear, some experts predict that in the future foods may be fortified with specific disease-preventing agents in the same way that today's foods are enhanced with VITAMINS and MINERALS. (See also VITAMIN B COMPLEX; VITAMIN C; VITAMIN E.)

► POTASSIUM

Sampling of Foods Rich in Potassium. *The recommended dietary allowance for potassium is 1,875 to 5,625 mg per day. Foods rich in this mineral include avocados, chili, bananas, and beef.*

Potassium is an essential MINERAL that is present in all living cells. Along with SODIUM, it helps carry the electrical charges that enable cells to function. Potassium helps maintain normal heart rhythm, the proper functioning of muscles, and the body's water balance. Although most foods contain potassium, the greatest quantities are found in vegetables (especially beans and potatoes), fruits (especially oranges and bananas), and whole grains.

Although the exact mechanism is unknown, potassium and sodium work together to affect blood pressure. Increasing the consumption of sodium (found in table SALT and most processed foods) is believed to raise blood pressure; increasing the amount of potassium in the diet appears to lower blood pressure by promoting the excretion of sodium.

Potassium Deficiency Because potassium is found in most foods, deficiencies are rare. However, they can occur with some digestive disorders and with continued diarrhea or vomiting, which results in the loss of potassium-rich fluids. Overconsumption of sugar, aspirin, coffee, or alcohol, as well as long-term treatment with certain drugs, can also deplete the body's supply of potassium. (See also RECOMMENDED DIETARY ALLOWANCE.)

▶ PRESIDENT'S COUNCIL ON PHYSICAL FITNESS AND SPORTS

The President's Council on Physical Fitness and Sports was established in 1956 to encourage FITNESS and sports participation among all Americans. The council uses advertising, articles, special events, and awards programs to focus public awareness on the importance of staying physically active. It also encourages schools, business and industry, government, recreation agencies, and sports and youth organizations to develop and maintain physical fitness and sports programs for people of all ages.

One of the major goals of the council is to help young Americans achieve fitness. One of its major programs is the *President's Challenge,* which motivates and rewards students aged 6 to 17 to meet challenging levels of fitness in cardiovascular and muscular endurance, strength, flexibility, and agility. (See also EXERCISE; FITNESS TRAINING; SPORTS AND FITNESS.)

▶ PROTEINS

Proteins are one of the three main groups of *macronutrients* (nutrients that the body needs in large amounts). Proteins are essential for the growth and repair of body tissues. Protein is a part of every cell and a key component in the structure of body tissues (such as hair, skin, muscles, tendons, and cartilage). Because protein is lost every day as cells wear out, it is needed in the diet daily.

The Composition of Proteins Proteins contain *amino acids,* chemicals that are referred to as the building blocks of the body. The body links the amino acids to form the proteins it needs.

Twenty-two amino acids build human proteins. Nine of them, called essential amino acids, must be supplied by food because the body cannot produce them. The body can manufacture the other 13 amino acids from substances in food. Because amino acids cannot be stored in the body, it is important to include them in your diet at least twice a day. Proteins can combine with SUGARS and BODY FAT to form more complex units.

HEALTHY CHOICES

Dietary Sources of Protein Foods of animal origin, such as meat, poultry, fish, milk products, and eggs, are *complete proteins* because they supply all nine essential amino acids. Plant foods, such as vegetables, seeds, grains, and nuts, also supply protein, but they usually lack one or more of the essential amino acids. Thus, they are called *incomplete proteins.* To get all of the essential amino acids from plant foods, you have to eat vegetable proteins with milk or eat combinations of food such as beans and rice. (See also VEGETARIAN DIET.)

HEALTHY CHOICES

Many protein-rich animal foods are high in FATS and low in FIBER. Therefore, you should try to get at least half of your daily protein requirements from plant food. Animal sources should be limited to lean meat and fish, poultry without skin, and low-fat or nonfat milk, yogurt, and cheeses (see chart: Sources of Protein).

The Role of Proteins in the Body Proteins play an important and complex role in many body processes. As discussed earlier, proteins in

SOURCES OF PROTEIN	
Low-fat proteins	**High-fat proteins**
Fish	Sausage, hot dogs, cold cuts
Poultry without skin	Eggs, especially the yolks
Lean meat	Peanut butter
Low-fat or nonfat milk	Most nuts and seeds
Buttermilk	Whole milk or cream
Low-fat or nonfat yogurt	Sour cream
Skimmed ricotta or mozzarella cheese	Ice cream
	Cheddar, Swiss, or blue cheese
	Cheese spreads

food are broken down by DIGESTION into amino acids, which become new body proteins. The genes in each cell direct each person's body to manufacture a different range of proteins. In fact, the differences in the "codes" that each person's genes contain for making proteins cause hereditary differences among people.

Proteins are either soluble or insoluble, and their role in the body depends on which type they are. *Insoluble proteins* (or fibrous proteins) form the structure of body tissues, such as hair, skin, muscles, tendons, and cartilage. *Soluble proteins* form the thousands of different body enzymes (substances that help speed up biochemical reactions in the body), hormones (chemical messengers that control body processes), and proteins in the blood. Blood proteins include hemoglobin, which carries oxygen to cells throughout the body for energy production, and antibodies, which help the body fight disease.

Soluble proteins also maintain several important balances within the body. Proteins in cells help regulate their mineral balance. Proteins in the blood help maintain fluid balance. Other soluble proteins help keep a specific pH balance in body systems.

Proteins also help regulate the nervous system. Two amino acids have been found to help transmit nerve impulses. Researchers are investigating how amino acids in the diet might affect behavior and the nervous system.

Finally, protein can be metabolized to produce energy. The body uses CARBOHYDRATES and fats for energy first, saving protein for more specialized uses. However, if there are not enough carbohydrates or fats for energy needs, the body uses protein for this purpose. (See also BODY METABOLISM; ENERGY, FOOD.)

Protein Requirements   Most young men need about 56 grams of protein every day, and young women need about 45 grams. As people age, they generally need less protein. The average American diet contains about 100 grams of protein daily, or about twice as much as is required. You can roughly calculate your protein needs by dividing your body weight by three. For example, a person who weighs 150 pounds will need about 50 grams of protein per day. This amount can be supplied by two 2- to 3-ounce (56- to 85-g) servings of lean meat, poultry, or fish.

RISK FACTORS
▶ ▶ ▶ ▶ ▶ ▶

Even a minor protein deficiency can cause FATIGUE and irritability. It also makes a person more prone to infection because of lowered antibody production. In addition, wounds will heal slowly, and recovery from illness will take longer. Prolonged protein deficiency may result in anemia or liver disorders.

Although protein is essential, too much is not beneficial. Excess proteins are usually converted to fatty acids and stored in fat tissue.

RISK FACTORS
▶ ▶ ▶ ▶ ▶ ▶

The average American diet generally provides more than enough protein. However, people who follow extreme weight loss diets or suffer from EATING DISORDERS, such as anorexia nervosa, can have protein deficiencies that eventually lead to MALNUTRITION. Malnutrition caused by protein deficiency is common in less developed countries. (See also FATS.)

RECOMMENDED DIETARY ALLOWANCE

The recommended dietary (or daily) allowance (RDA) is an estimate of the amount of essential NUTRIENTS that the average healthy person should consume daily to maintain good health. RDAs are listed on many food packages to provide consumers with information on the nutrients contained in one serving of the food.

Different countries compute RDAs or their equivalents using different methods. The *U.S. RDA* for PROTEIN and 19 VITAMINS and MINERALS is established by the Food and Nutrition Board of the National Research Council, a part of the National Academy of Sciences. Reviewed every 5 years, the board's recommendations are provided as nutritional guidelines. The amounts specified for daily intake are not minimum figures; they are set on the high side.

Because nutritional needs vary by age and sex, so do RDAs. In addition, the special dietary requirements of pregnant and nursing women are

RDAs on Food Labels. *The RDAs listed on food labels are a useful tool for comparing the relative nutritional value of similar foods.*

SODIUM, mg
POTASSIUM, mg | 110 | 310

PERCENTAGE OF U.S. RECOMMENDED DAILY ALLOWANCES (U.S. RDA)

PROTEIN	4	10
VITAMIN A	25	30
VITAMIN C	25	25
THIAMIN	25	30
RIBOFLAVIN	25	35
NIACIN	25	25
CALCIUM	6	20
IRON	45	45
VITAMIN D	10	25
VITAMIN B₆	25	25
FOLIC ACID	25	25
PHOSPHORUS	10	20
MAGNESIUM	8	10
ZINC	4	6
COPPER	4	4

INGREDIENTS: WHOLE WHEAT, SUGAR, SALT, MALT EXTRACT, CORN SYRUP, CALCIUM CARBONATE, CALCIUM CHLORIDE, TRISODIUM PHOSPHATE, VITAMIN C (SODIUM ASCORBATE), IRON (A MINERAL NUTRIENT), A B VITAMIN (NIACINAMIDE), VITAMIN A (PALMITATE), VITAMIN B₆ (PYRIDOXINE

allowed for. Even within these specific groups, however, the needs of individuals vary. Probably the best way to obtain RDAs in your diet is to eat a variety of healthful foods.

You should also remember that RDAs are for healthy people only. Illness and disease can increase the body's needs for certain nutrients.

On food labels, the RDA for each nutrient is expressed as a percentage (see illustration: RDAs on Food Labels). For example, the label on a cereal box may say that one serving of the cereal provides 25 percent of the RDA of vitamin A.

If a nutrient is added to a food product or if the manufacturer makes a claim about the product, such as that it is low in calories or high in vitamin C, federal law requires information about the RDA of protein and 7 other vitamins and minerals to be listed on the package. Manufacturers have the option of including RDA information about the 12 other nutrients as well, and many do. (See also DIETARY GUIDELINES; FOOD LABELING.)

► REST

Rest is physical and mental relaxation that helps overcome FATIGUE, reduces stress, and restores energy to the body. Adequate rest, including periods of sleep and relaxation, is an important part of a healthy LIFESTYLE. Without enough rest, a person feels tired, lacks concentration, and loses efficiency in physical and mental tasks.

Sleep   Sleep allows the body and mind to rest. During sleep, BODY METABOLISM, HEART RATE, and breathing become slower, and body temperature drops. Although requirements differ for each individual, most adults need between 7 and 8½ hours of sleep every day.

Relaxation   Relaxation involves reducing physical and mental tension and can help reduce *stress*. A sense of physical relaxation often occurs after vigorous exercise, such as jogging or participating in an active sport.

Relaxation. *Taking a short break from your work or switching to a different activity can help you relax.*

Relaxation can also be achieved through any of four specific techniques: breathing exercises, progressive muscle relaxation, biofeedback, and meditation.

Breathing exercises use slow, deep breaths that emphasize exhaling slowly and gently. These exercises can be performed to aid in relaxation whenever feelings of stress occur. *Progressive muscle relaxation* alternately tenses and relaxes muscle groups, working progressively (from the feet to the head, for instance) until the whole body is relaxed. A quiet room, a comfortable mat or mattress, and soothing background music can enhance muscle relaxation. *Biofeedback* uses monitoring devices to detect activity and tension within the body. An enhanced awareness of the body can aid relaxation and tension reduction. As an example, one biofeedback method uses small electrodes on the skin of the forehead to monitor muscle tension. This provides feedback on whether relaxation techniques are successful in relaxing muscles. *Meditation* helps achieve a relaxed mind and body by combining physical relaxation with concentration on an image or repetitive thought (a mantra) to help block out distracting thoughts and other stimuli.

HEALTHY CHOICES

Try to include periods of relaxation in your day. Even a change of pace—something as simple as switching to a different activity for a short time—can help you relax.

Recuperation   Extra rest is normally beneficial to anyone recuperating from illness or injury. A day or two of rest is recommended for most minor sports injuries, for example, followed by a gradual return to activity that gently exercises the injured area. Activity increases blood flow, which speeds healing and helps prevent muscles from weakening and joints from getting stiff. More serious injuries or illnesses may require longer periods of rest to allow the body to heal itself. (See also ENERGY, PHYSICAL; SLEEP, 1; RELAXATION TRAINING, 5; SLEEP PROBLEMS, 5; STRESS-MANAGEMENT TECHNIQUES, 5.)

▶ **RISK FACTORS**   Risk factors are characteristics or behaviors that increase the likelihood of medical disorders or disease. Some risk factors, such as age, sex, race, and hereditary characteristics, are beyond an individual's control. However, others, such as environment and lifestyle, are largely controllable.

Risk Factors That Cannot Be Controlled   The traits and qualities that people inherit from their parents are beyond their control. One of those traits is the tendency to develop certain diseases. For example, a person whose mother and father had heart disease or cancer has a greater chance of developing that disease than does a person who has no such family history.

People cannot do anything to reduce inherited risk factors. However, if they are aware of these inherited tendencies, they can work at controlling other risk factors such as environment and lifestyle.

Risk Factors That Can Be Controlled   A person's environment is controllable for the most part. For example, although people cannot

Risk Factors. *Cigarette smoking is a behavioral risk factor that contributes directly to lung cancer, heart disease, and other illnesses.*

change the air they breathe, they can move out of a neighborhood or region that has poor air quality.

LIFESTYLE is the risk factor that is most controllable. It is also a critical factor in determining health. The way people live can greatly increase or decrease their chances of developing diseases. For example, heart disease actually has its roots in lifestyle. Behaviors such as smoking cigarettes, eating a diet high in saturated FATS and CHOLESTEROL, and failing to EXERCISE regularly contribute to heart disease. The greater the number of these risk factors, the greater the chances of contracting the disease.

Many diseases, including many forms of cancer and diabetes, have risk factors that are based on behaviors and habits, especially those relating to *diet* and *exercise*. With a little knowledge and effort, people can reduce or entirely eliminate many risk factors. Appropriate changes in environment and lifestyle can significantly reduce the chances of contracting a serious disease.

Controlling Risk Factors   An awareness of the risk factors for various diseases is the first step toward making behavioral changes that can reduce the likelihood of a disease. For instance, by knowing that cigarette smoking, a high-fat diet, and excessive alcohol consumption are major risk factors in cancer, a person can choose to stop smoking, eat a low-fat diet, and keep drinking to a minimum in order to lessen the chances of developing it.

People who already have a disease can also take steps to control risk factors that could make it worse. For example, people who have diabetes can control their diet and weight and avoid smoking. If they do not control those risk factors, their disease will probably get much worse. (See also FITNESS; MALNUTRITION; OBESITY; HEREDITY AND ENVIRONMENT, **5**.)

▷ **RUNNING**

Running is one of the most popular exercise activities in the United States. Anyone in good health can run; it requires no special equipment except for a good pair of running shoes. A form of AEROBIC EXERCISE, running activities improve the fitness of the heart and lungs and strengthen the muscles of the lower body. Participation in running varies from casually jogging short distances around the neighborhood to competing in 26.2-mile (42.2-km) *marathon* races.

HEALTHY CHOICES

Benefits of Running   Running is one of the most effective exercises for burning calories and reducing weight. A runner can expend 400 or more calories in half an hour. The positive effects of a regular running program include lower blood pressure and a slower heart rate. These effects can be achieved by a half-hour run taken 3 or 4 days each week. Regular running also adds some muscle mass and substantially decreases the amount of body fat. (See also BODY COMPOSITION.)

Preparing to Run   Begin a running program by taking brisk walks for 30 to 45 minutes three times a week. Move on to alternating walking with running, gradually increasing the amount of time spent running. Begin each running session with 5 to 10 minutes of warm-up and STRETCHING EXERCISES to loosen muscles. End each session with a cool-down

Clothing for Running. *If running where there is traffic, wear bright-colored clothing. If running at night, wear clothing with reflective strips that can be seen easily.*

period of brisk walking to allow your blood pressure and heart rate to return to preexercise levels.

A runner's most important purchase is a pair of high-quality running shoes. Running shoes should feel comfortable and give good support. Especially important are a well-cushioned heel, a flexible midsole, and plenty of room above the toe. If your foot is between sizes, buy the size that is slightly too big. If your foot rolls inward (pronation) or outward (supination) too much, pain and injuries can result. Special devices (called orthotics) prescribed by foot doctors can help correct foot roll. (See also ATHLETIC FOOTWEAR.)

Running Safety Runners put a great deal of stress on their legs, knees, and feet. Most injuries can be prevented by wearing the proper footwear, avoiding hard or uneven running surfaces, and increasing running time gradually. The most common injuries are blisters, ankle sprains, shin splints (pain in the shins), and muscle pulls and cramps.

Pay attention to the body's signals, and give injuries time to heal. Any pain or tenderness that does not clear up or that recurs should be investigated by a specialist in SPORTS MEDICINE or an orthopedist (bone doctor). (See also ENDURANCE; FITNESS; HEART RATE; SPORTS INJURIES.)

▶ SALT

Salt, or *sodium chloride,* is a mineral that is widely used to season and preserve foods. Essential to good health, salt helps to balance the level of water and *electrolytes* (substances that carry nerve impulses) in the body and enables cells to function normally. *Salt* commonly means table salt, but in chemical terms, a salt is formed when an *acid* reacts with a *base*.

Most table salt is iodized, meaning it contains small amounts of *iodine*. Iodine is added to prevent a condition called *goiter,* which is an enlargement of the thyroid gland resulting from a lack of iodine.

Most Americans add salt to many foods. From a nutritional standpoint, doing so is undesirable because most Americans consume too

Unsalty Snacks. *Many traditionally salty foods are now available in salt-free varieties.*

RISK FACTORS
▶ ▶ ▶ ▶ ▶ ▶

HEALTHY CHOICES
●●●●●●●●●●●●

much salt. Too much SODIUM causes the body to retain fluids, which can result in *hypertension,* or high blood pressure. In order to reduce sodium intake, many people substitute seasonings that do not contain sodium. (See also MINERALS; MONOSODIUM GLUTAMATE; POTASSIUM; HYPERTENSION, **3.**)

▶ SNACK FOOD

Snack food is any food that people eat between meals. Snack foods provide people with energy, but they differ greatly in their nutritional value and the amount of energy they provide.

Types of Snack Food   When people think of snack food, they usually think of quick, ready-to-eat, packaged foods that are typically high in CALORIES, FATS, SALT, and SUGAR, and low in NUTRIENTS; the low nutrient content and high calorie content is why the calories from these foods are called empty calories. These foods include potato chips, salted pretzels, candy, cookies, and soft drinks. Many snack foods provide only short-term energy. Shortly after eating them, people feel hungry again.

HEALTHY CHOICES
●●●●●●●●●●●●

Snack food that is nutritious is a better choice because it supplies people with nutrients as well as energy. Quick, ready-to-eat snacks that are relatively healthful include fresh fruits, raw vegetables, nuts, seeds, cereal, yogurt, cheese slices, and unbuttered popcorn. Although some of these are high in fats, they provide more VITAMINS, MINERALS, CARBOHY-DRATES, and PROTEINS than do most typical snack foods. Fruits, vegetables, and grains also contain FIBER, which fills you up and satisfies your AP-PETITE until your next meal.

HEALTHY CHOICES
●●●●●●●●●●●●

Guidelines for Snacking   Snack foods can be part of a balanced diet as long as you choose nutritious snacks most of the time and eat them in moderation. When selecting prepared, prepackaged foods, choose baked snacks such as unsalted pretzels instead of fried snacks such as potato chips. Look for foods that are made from whole-grain flour instead of white flour.

Always read the nutrition label on packaged products to determine how many calories they contain and how many of those calories come from fat. Many snacks that claim to be low-calorie or "light" are actually high in salt, fat, and calories. (See also FOOD LABELING.)

Although the quality of the food you eat is most important, be aware of the quantity as well. Eating snack food all evening after having three balanced meals will almost certainly cause a weight gain. There-fore, it is important to remember to include snack food as part of the to-tal calories allowed each day. (See also FAST FOOD; JUNK FOOD; WEIGHT MANAGEMENT.)

▶ SODIUM

Sodium is an essential MINERAL that performs a number of important functions in the body. Along with POTASSIUM and other substances, it helps transport electric charges between nerves and muscles and main-tains a balance of fluids in the body. Sodium is also involved in the

High Sodium Content in Processed Foods. *Foods that are high in sodium do not always taste salty, so a salt-conscious consumer should check food labels.*

proper functioning of muscles, including the heart. Although sodium is most familiar as the main ingredient of table SALT, it is contained in almost all natural and processed foods.

The main forms of sodium found in food are *sodium chloride* (table salt), *sodium bicarbonate* (baking soda), and MONOSODIUM GLUTAMATE (MSG), a widely used flavoring in Chinese and other foods. Large amounts of sodium are also present in many foods, including cheeses, breads and cereals, cured and smoked meats, pickles, bacon, and snack foods. Processed and packaged foods tend to be especially high in sodium, even when they do not taste particularly salty. Catsup is just one example. Sodium also occurs naturally in vegetables such as spinach, celery, beets, carrots, and cabbage. Some drugs, including many *laxatives* and *sedatives,* also contain sodium, as does drinking water treated with softeners.

Because sodium is found in almost all foods, most Americans consume much more than they need (see illustration: High Sodium Content in Processed Foods). In fact, the average American consumes two to three times the recommended amount each day. Too much sodium in the diet can cause the body to retain water, and in some people this can result in dizziness and swelling of the legs. It may also increase the risk of *hypertension,* or high blood pressure, especially in people with a hereditary tendency to develop the disease, although this conclusion is under increasing challenge.

RISK FACTORS
▶ ▶ ▶ ▶ ▶ ▶

Sodium deficiency can also be dangerous. Persistent diarrhea or vomiting, excessive sweating, kidney disease, disorders of the adrenal glands, and prolonged treatment with *diuretic drugs* (which increase the output of urine) can all result in sodium loss.

HEALTHY CHOICES
■•••••••••••••

No official RECOMMENDED DIETARY ALLOWANCE has been established for sodium. The average adult, however, should consume no more than 5 grams (about 2 teaspoons) per day. This includes both salt contained in foods and table salt added to foods at home. People with high blood pressure, kidney or liver disease, or edema (an abnormal fluid buildup in the body) as well as those at risk for these conditions should follow a *low-salt diet*. Foods low in salt include skim milk, eggs, poultry, fish, fresh fruits, salad, asparagus, broccoli, and green beans. Salt-conscious consumers should also be sure to check the sodium content listed on the nutrition labels of most foods and take the salt shaker off the table—herbs and spices can be used to provide just as much flavor as table salt. (See also CALCIUM; VITAMINS; WATER; HYPERTENSION, **3.**)

▶ **SPORTS AND FITNESS** Sports and fitness are interrelated. Fitness improves performance levels in most sports; regular participation in most sports improves fitness by one or more of several basic measures. The primary measures of FITNESS include STRENGTH, muscular and cardiovascular ENDURANCE, and FLEXIBILITY. The nature and degree of fitness benefits vary by each sport and by the level at which a sport is played.

Choosing a Sport For the competitive athlete, excellence and victory are the goals of sports. For most people, however, improving fitness, having fun with friends, and enjoying competing and winning are the goals of sports. People who exercise to achieve fitness should choose a sport they enjoy that also matches their fitness goals. For example, for *cardiovascular endurance* and strength, CYCLING, SWIMMING, and roller skating are good choices. If strength and flexibility are the goals, gymnastics and karate are among the better choices.

The choice of a sport will also depend on many other factors, including your body type, fitness level, personality, and the climate where you live. In addition, you will want to find a sport that fits your schedule and that you can afford.

SPORTS AND FITNESS REQUIREMENTS

Sport	Aerobic fitness	Upper-body strength	Lower-body strength	Muscle endurance	Flexibility
Baseball	1	2	2	1	3
Basketball	4	2	2	2	4
Football, touch	2	2	2	2	3
Golf	2	1	1	1	2
Hockey	4	3	3	2	3
Martial arts	4	4	3	3	4
Skiing, downhill	3	2	3	4	3
Soccer	4	2	2	2	3
Tennis	3	1	2	1	3
Volleyball	2	2	2	2	3

Scale: 1=low; 2=moderate; 3=above average; 4=high

If your sport of choice is seasonal, you might want to take up a second in order to stay fit all year. For instance, you might cross-country ski in the winter and play tennis during the rest of the year. A mix of enjoyable activities provides variety and helps you stay challenged and interested. In addition, if you choose sports with different fitness elements, your fitness will be more balanced. You will also place less stress on any single part of your body, minimizing your chance of injury.

Individual Sports   Some people prefer individual sports, those played alone or with one or two others. They may enjoy the solitude of rowing after a hectic day or the challenge of trying to better their last golf score.

Individual sports come in many varieties and offer different fitness benefits. For example, AEROBIC DANCE, martial arts, RUNNING, cross-country skiing, and brisk WALKING all build cardiovascular fitness. In addition, martial arts build strength and flexibility; the others build *muscular endurance*. Strength is the major fitness benefit of downhill skiing and weight lifting.

Team Sports   Some people prefer team sports. They may enjoy the strategy, competition, and teamwork involved or the camaraderie associated with practices and games.

The fitness benefits of team sports vary. For example, basketball, ice hockey, field hockey, lacrosse, racquetball, and soccer build cardiovascular and muscular endurance as well as flexibility. Football builds strength; baseball and softball build strength and flexibility. Many team sports mix rapid bursts of intense energy with periods of lower intensity.

Getting Started   Whether you choose an individual or team sport, you have to plan and organize your fitness effort. How you begin depends on your level of fitness, how skilled you already are at the sport, the demands the sport makes on your body, and the need for equipment, partners, team members, or a coach. For example, touch football does not require much skill or equipment, but you have to have enough people to make up teams. Fencing, on the other hand, demands a high level of cardiovascular fitness and skill as well as special equipment and a partner.

Training for Sports   Before you can train for a sport, you need to analyze its fitness requirements (see chart: Sports and Fitness Requirements). For example, football and baseball require a high level of upper-body strength so training for those sports places emphasis on building that area. Sports like basketball and hockey that demand a great deal of cardiovascular endurance would call for training like AEROBIC EXERCISE to improve the body's ability to sustain activity.

After you have analyzed a sport's fitness requirements, you need to begin practicing and training. Practicing improves skills that are specific to your sport, such as dribbling in basketball. Training improves fitness levels so you are better able to excel at any sport. One of the keys to effective training is three good aerobic workouts a week. You should also add STRENGTH EXERCISES and STRETCHING EXERCISES. These build overall strength and flexibility and reduce your chances of a sports-related injury.

When you practice or train, be sure to include warm-up sessions so your muscles are warm and loose. Afterward, cool down to help avoid soreness and aches. As a general rule, make stretching exercises part of

> The fitness benefits of team sports vary. Basketball and soccer, for example, build cardiovascular endurance and flexibility. Hockey builds upper and lower body strength.

every warm-up and cool-down. (See also FITNESS TRAINING; SPORTS INJURIES.)

▶ **SPORTS AND HEAT PROBLEMS** A variety of health problems can result from EXERCISE in hot or humid weather. When air temperature approaches body temperature or when high humidity saturates the air with water, the body is less able to cool itself adequately. Direct sunlight on the skin may also raise body heat. An overheated body can produce a variety of heat-related conditions threatening to health, some serious.

Types of Medical Problems Among the medical problems heat may cause are dehydration, heat cramps, heat exhaustion, and heatstroke.

Intensive sweating during exercise can cause DEHYDRATION. This excessive decrease in the levels of body fluids can lead to dizziness, nausea, weakness, and even death.

Exercising in hot or humid weather may also bring on *heat cramps*, painful muscle spasms that are caused by an imbalance of fluids and salts in the body. Heat cramps may occur during or after a workout.

Heat exhaustion is a more serious problem that results from a heavy loss of fluids and salts due to profuse sweating. Symptoms of heat exhaustion include red and flushed skin, FATIGUE, rapid breathing, weakness, dizziness, and nausea. To relieve these symptoms, stop exercising, rest in a cool, dry place, and drink large amounts of cool liquids to bring your temperature down. A cool bath or shower may also be helpful.

Untreated heat exhaustion may progress to *heatstroke,* an acute medical emergency that occurs when the body's cooling mechanisms break down completely and body temperature rises rapidly. Heatstroke may be caused by strenuous exercise in hot or humid weather.

One of the first symptoms of heatstroke is that sweating stops and the skin becomes dry and very hot. Lacking the cooling effect of PERSPIRATION, the body temperature can rise quickly to 106°F (41.1°C) or more.

RISK FACTORS
▶ ▶ ▶ ▶ ▶ ▶

Working Out in the Heat.
Coaches of organized sports have to monitor weather conditions during summer workouts and be attentive to signs of heat-related problems in their athletes.

This excessive body temperature can damage the brain, heart, and other organs. Other symptoms of heatstroke include grogginess, confusion, collapse, and, eventually, coma. Low levels of body fluids may upset blood chemistry, leading to kidney failure, liver damage, and blood clotting abnormalities. Heatstroke requires medical treatment immediately. Until assistance arrives, a person suspected of having heatstroke should be moved out of the sun and into a cool place and have cold compresses or ice packs applied to the body. (See also HEATSTROKE, 8.)

Preventing Heat-Related Problems   The key to preventing heat-related sports problems is to use common sense when exercising in weather that is significantly hotter or more humid than what you are used to. First, it is essential to drink liquids before, during, and after any hot-weather workout to replace fluid lost in sweating. WATER is good enough, although some people prefer drinks that are designed for athletic fluid replacement. Second, stay alert to the early symptoms of heat-related problems, which can warn of a serious developing medical condition.

HEALTHY CHOICES

In hot weather, an exercise such as SWIMMING that is unlikely to produce overheating may be preferred. If you really want to run or play tennis when it is hot, however, it may be wise to shorten your workout or to exercise during the cooler early morning or evening hours.

▶ **SPORTS INJURIES**   Sports injuries are those that result from exercising or participating in sports. The chances of injury vary from sport to sport and with the level of competition. The more physical strain a sport places on the body, the more likely a sports injury becomes. In addition, the nature of individual sports makes certain kinds of injuries more likely than others. Runners, for example, tend to injure feet, ankles, and legs, whereas tennis players frequently injure elbows. Typical or not, all injuries resulting from athletics are classified as sports injuries, and their treatment depends on their nature and severity.

Treating Common Sports Injuries   Many mild sports injuries, including muscle strains and pulls, bruises, and sprains, can be treated at home with a simple first-aid routine called RICE. RICE stands for Rest, Ice the injured area to prevent swelling, Compress the injured area with a bandage, and Elevate the injured area above the level of the heart to help fluids drain. Treat moderate injuries with the RICE process for 48 hours. If the injury does not improve in that time, consult a physician. Do not attempt to treat severe sports injuries and serious SPORTS AND HEAT PROBLEMS, such as heat exhaustion and heatstroke. Instead, contact a physician immediately.

CONSULT A
PHYSICIAN

The following list includes some of the most common sports injuries and how to treat them.

> ▶ *Back pain* and injuries are a risk in many sports. Medical treatments may include medications to relieve pain and relax muscles, heat treatments, and use of a neck brace. (See also BACK PROBLEMS, 3.)

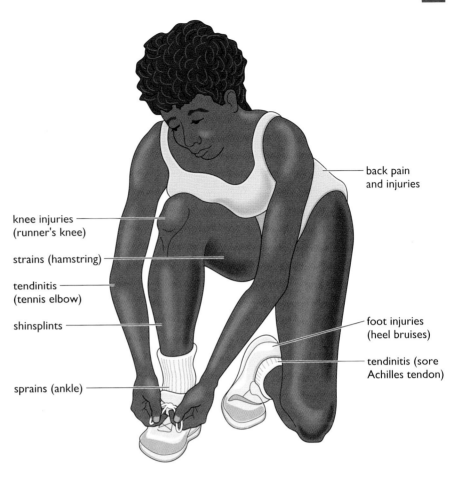

back pain
and injuries

knee injuries
(runner's knee)

strains (hamstring)

tendinitis
(tennis elbow)

shinsplints

foot injuries
(heel bruises)

tendinitis (sore
Achilles tendon)

sprains (ankle)

Common Sports Injuries.

▸ *Blisters* form as a result of friction against the skin. They often occur on the foot. A blister should be covered with a thick bandage or blister pad. Treat broken blisters with an antiseptic. Never break a blister on purpose. (See also BLISTER, **3.**)

▸ *Bruises* result from an impact that causes bleeding under the skin. Treat them by using the RICE process. If pain persists for 3 days, see a physician.

▸ *Chafing* is raw and irritated skin. It occurs frequently in the groin area. Treat chafing with a medicated powder, and prevent further problems by wearing clothing made from cotton.

▸ *Cramps* are caused by muscle spasms and are more likely when the athlete has not warmed up completely before exercising. If a cramp occurs, stop exercising right away, stretch the muscle, and drink plenty of fluids.

▸ *Foot injuries,* such as heel bruises, are usually caused by sudden and severe impact of the foot on a hard surface. To treat them, use the RICE process. For heel bruises, wear a heel pad when putting weight on the heel again. (See also FOOT PROBLEMS, **3.**)

▸ *Knee injuries,* such as runner's knee, a dull, aching pain caused by overuse, require rest and, in many cases, specialized medical care.

▸ *Lacerations* and *abrasions,* commonly referred to as cuts and scrapes, can often be treated with simple first aid. Wash the affected area with an antiseptic, and cover it with a bandage or dressing. A tetanus shot may be necessary if dirt or other foreign matter has entered the wound. If the injury is severe or if an infection develops, see a physician. (See also TETANUS, **2**; INJURIES, **8**.)

► *Shinsplints* are an aching pain on the front of the lower legs. This is a common problem that is often caused by incorrect movements, poor shoes, or a very hard exercise surface. Shinsplints usually improve with rest.

► *Sore muscles* often occur 8 to 10 hours after strenuous exercise. To treat them, keep muscles moving with slow, easy stretches. You can relieve the pain with acetaminophen, warm baths, and massage.

► *Sprains* and *strains* can be mild to severe. Mild sprains and strains cause tenderness but no swelling and can be treated with the RICE process. Moderate sprains and strains limit function and cause tenderness, pain, swelling, discoloration, and possible muscle spasms. Use the RICE process at first. If the affected area has not improved after 24 to 72 hours, see a physician. For severe sprains and strains, call a physician immediately. (See also SPRAINS AND STRAINS, **8**.)

► *Tendinitis,* or inflamed tendons, often affects the Achilles tendon behind the ankle, the shoulder joint, and the elbow (resulting in tennis elbow). Treatment includes using the RICE process and resting for up to a few weeks until the pain subsides. See a physician if you think you might have torn a tendon or if you have had repeated problems with tendinitis. (See also TENDINITIS, **3**.)

Tips for Preventing Sports Injuries Many injuries that occur as a result of exercise can be prevented. A large proportion of sports injuries are the result of participating too little or too often or increasing training level too fast. Weekend athletes, for example, who have no regular FITNESS routine frequently overextend themselves when they do play a sport—and get hurt as a result. At the other extreme, competitive athletes need to be careful not to risk injury as the result of overtraining. Moderation is a key to avoiding sports injuries.

Be realistic about how much you can do when you begin a sport or exercise regimen. Assess your physical ability and condition and choose activities that suit your body. For example, someone with bad knees should not take up CYCLING or soccer.

Learn as much as you can about the injury risks of the sports you take part in. Some sports, such as football, soccer, and basketball, that are popular with young people can be hard on joints and lead to problems and injuries later in life. Be sure to use any special safety equipment required. Many sports require, for instance, that people wear good shock-absorbing shoes to prevent pain and injuries. Always buy the highest-quality equipment that you can afford. In addition, select appropriate places to exercise. For example, a resilient surface is important for cushioning the impact of running, jumping, or doing aerobics.

Condition your body thoroughly by planning a balanced EXERCISE program. In addition, focus on building strong muscles around the joints that receive the most strain in your sport. If you experience pain at any time during your workout, stop immediately and rest.

Warm up and stretch muscles thoroughly for at least 10 minutes before exercising. This increases the temperature of your muscles so they are more flexible and harder to injure. After exercising, cool down gradually to let your HEART RATE and body return to a resting state.

RISK FACTORS
▶ ▶ ▶ ▶ ▶ ▶

Try to avoid extremes in temperature. Strenuous exercise during hot, humid weather can lead to heatstroke or other heat-related problems, and in cold weather, muscles pull more easily. (See also ATHLETIC FOOTWEAR; SPORTS MEDICINE; STRENGTH EXERCISE; STRETCHING EXERCISE; PAIN, 3; FIRST AID, 8; RICE, 8.)

▷ **SPORTS MEDICINE**   Sports medicine is a rapidly growing medical field that specializes in improving FITNESS, treating and preventing SPORTS INJURIES, and providing physical rehabilitation for injured athletes. Treatment of an injury may include exercise programs, nutritional advice, fitness tests, or surgery to repair damaged tissues.

Sports Medicine Specialists   The first sports medicine specialists were team physicians who provided medical care for amateur and professional sports teams. Today, many sports medicine specialists operate *sports medicine clinics* where both team athletes and those who engage in individual sports, such as RUNNING, CYCLING, or WEIGHT TRAINING, can seek treatment for injuries.

The need for sports medicine specialists stems from the fact that the physical demands of specific sports tend to cause specific kinds of injuries. The torn rotator cuff muscles in the shoulders of baseball pitchers and torn knee ligaments of running backs in football are just two common examples. Some injuries are so associated with a sport that they take their name from it, as in runner's knee and tennis elbow. Many of these injuries and conditions are rare in nonathletes and may be unfamiliar to the nonspecialist.

Many sports medicine practitioners are *orthopedists* or orthopedic surgeons, specialists in treating disorders of the musculoskeletal system.

Treating Sports Injuries. *In a sports medicine clinic, one or more specialists may advise an athlete about healing an injury or preventing future problems.*

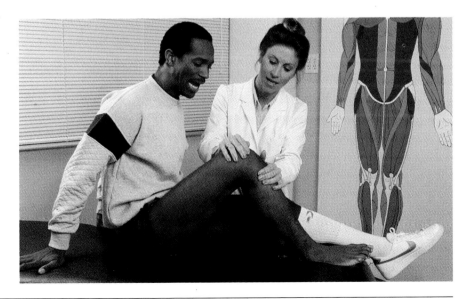

Some *podiatrists* (foot specialists) also treat athletes. Along with orthopedists, they may provide advice on ATHLETIC FOOTWEAR and prescribe *orthotic devices*. These are foam, leather, or plastic inserts worn in the shoe to correct foot abnormalities. Physical therapists and athletic trainers plan exercise and treatment programs for injured athletes. A relatively new type of sports medicine practitioners, *sports psychologists,* deal with the mental aspects of athletic performance.

Treating and Preventing Sports Injuries Most competitive athletes want to continue to participate in their sport while their injuries are healing. When athletes must take a break from their sport, treatment may include alternative forms of activity so the athletes can keep fit while resting the injured body part. An injured runner, for example, might row, swim, or lift weights while a leg injury heals.

An important emphasis in sports medicine is the building of strength, endurance, and flexibility as a means of preventing sports injuries. Clinic physicians also provide advice about clothing, equipment, and technique to help athletes avoid injuries. (See also PHYSICAL THERAPIST, **9**; PHYSICIANS (M.D.'s)—ORTHOPEDIST, **9**; PODIATRIST, **9**.)

▶ STARCH

Starch is one of the three types of CARBOHYDRATES, one that the body needs in large amounts. The other two are SUGAR and FIBER. Starches are NUTRIENTS that consist of a long chemical chain of as many as 3,000 glucose molecules. Although each GLUCOSE molecule is itself a sugar (a *simple carbohydrate*), linked together they become *complex carbohydrates.*

Nutritional Value of Starch Complex carbohydrates are excellent foods for two distinct reasons. First, they produce energy for the body in

Foods High in Starch. *Nutrition experts recommend that 50 percent of total daily calories come from complex carbohydrates such as starch.*

a form that is broken down more slowly than simple carbohydrates. More important, starchy foods, which are entirely of plant origin, are usually rich in VITAMINS, MINERALS, PROTEINS, and fiber and low in CALORIES and FAT. For these reasons, nutritionists recommend that 40 to 50 percent of a person's caloric intake be in the form of starches.

During the digestive process, starches are broken down into simple sugars called *monosaccharides*. These are absorbed by the body and converted into glucose, the fuel of cell metabolism. If there is excess glucose, a small amount is stored in the liver and muscles for later use. The remainder is converted into fat.

Sources of Starch   The best source of starch is grains, such as rice, wheat, and corn. The legume family (beans and peas) and the tuber family (potatoes, yams, and cassava) are also good sources of starch (see illustration: Foods High in Starch). (See also BREADS AND CEREALS GROUP; ENERGY, FOOD.)

▶ STRENGTH

Strength Conditioning.
Strength is an important part of fitness. Developing upper-body strength, for example, can greatly improve the performance of long-distance runners.

Strength is a basic element of muscular fitness. Strength helps the body meet the physical demands of everyday life. Adequate strength helps prevent injuries, reduces muscle aches and pains, and improves posture, among other benefits. Strength, FLEXIBILITY, and muscular and cardiovascular ENDURANCE are the basic elements of physical FITNESS.

Strength can be increased with regular EXERCISE that places demands on muscles. When muscles work hard against resistance, they break down slightly, then rebuild themselves, becoming larger and stronger. Without regular exercise, however, strength decreases, and muscles *atrophy*, or grow smaller, especially as an adult grows older.

Measuring Strength   Strength is the amount of force muscles can exert against resistance. Specific exercises are a simple way to measure overall strength. For example, push-ups test the strength of chest and arm muscles, and the number that can be done is an indication of their strength. The amount of weight a person can lift can also be used to measure strength.

Increasing Strength   An exercise program that places progressively greater resistance against muscles will build strength. Working with weights, either EXERCISE MACHINES or free weights, is a common and effective method of improving strength.

Strength training requires regular workouts—usually three times a week with at least a day of rest between workouts to prevent muscle fatigue, soreness, and injury. Generally, strength exercises are performed in "sets" of 8 to 12 repetitions of an exercise that places a great deal of resistance against a specific muscle group. With regular repetition, muscles should respond to this kind of training by becoming stronger, which should make the exercise become easier. When it does, increase the amount of resistance (usually in the form of weight or the number of repetitions) used in the exercise. This keeps the muscles working hard, which is the key to building strength. (See also STRENGTH EXERCISE; WEIGHT TRAINING.)

▷ **STRENGTH EXERCISE** Strength exercise is exercise that builds up the muscles and increases the body's ability to perform work. All strength exercises are movements that force a muscle or muscle group to contract against resistance—for example, by lifting a weight. In strength exercise, the muscles are pushed to their maximum or near maximum. This process is called *overload*. Demanding progressively more from the muscles causes them to increase in size and STRENGTH. The three basic kinds of strength exercise are isometric exercise, isotonic exercise, and isokinetic exercise.

Isometric Exercise In isometric exercise, a person pushes against an immovable object, such as a wall or doorway, or pushes muscle groups against each other. Each muscle contraction is held for 5 to 8 seconds, and then the muscle is relaxed. Isometric exercise is out of favor as a means of developing overall strength because it exercises a muscle only in one position; also it raises blood pressure in some individuals. Isometric exercise can be useful, however, for people who want to build strength at a specific point in the range of motion. It is often used for rehabilitation after a joint injury. In this type of exercise, the joint does not move and is therefore not stressed.

Isotonic Exercise Isotonic exercise includes many exercises that are performed in calisthenics, such as push-ups and chin-ups, as well as in weight lifting. This type of exercise works by making a muscle push a weight through a range of motion. To increase strength most efficiently, the weight should be near the maximum a person can push or lift, and the number of repetitions should be kept low.

Isokinetic Exercise Isokinetic exercise also requires muscles to lift a weight through a range of motion. The exercise is performed, however, on special machines (such as some Cybex machines) that use cables, pulleys, and weights to control the speed of the motion throughout the exercise. In this way the machine keeps a maximum load on the muscle throughout its movement.

Types of Strength Exercise.
Weight lifting is a type of isotonic exercise in which the arm muscles lift weights as they move through a range of motion. Isokinetic exercise works in a similar way but uses special machines.

Using Strength Exercise Some kinds of strength exercise—especially calisthenics, weight lifting, and isometrics—lend themselves to being performed at home using no special equipment or fairly inexpensive equipment (such as dumbbells or barbells). Lifting heavy weights, however,

should not be done alone. Exercise with a partner to prevent injury. Because most strength-building machines are expensive, joining a health club, recreation center, or gym may be necessary. Also, remember that strength exercise does little to improve the function of the heart and lungs. It should be combined with AEROBIC EXERCISE and STRETCHING EXERCISE to attain maximum FITNESS. (See also BODY BUILDING.)

▷ STRETCHING EXERCISE

Stretching exercise is movement designed to relieve muscle tension and increase FLEXIBILITY. It increases the blood supply to the muscles and other tissues, making them more supple and efficient, which helps prevent injuries such as tears and sprains. Stretching exercise should always be a part of the warm-up and cool-down activities performed before and after other kinds of exercises. By relaxing tight, bunched muscles, stretching is also a good way for people who get little exercise to improve posture, relieve muscle pain, and even manage stress.

Stretching Exercises. (a) *In this one type of* static stretching *exercise, keep the knees bent and roll down until the hamstring and back muscles begin to pull. Hold for a few seconds, then release.* (b) *This* contract-relax stretching *exercise can be done with a partner. The person lying down pushes the leg down against the partner's shoulder and holds it there for a few seconds, contracting the hamstrings. The person then pulls the leg back toward the head. This relaxes the hamstrings and contracts the quadriceps.*

Types of Stretching Exercise

There are three basic types of stretching techniques.

- In *ballistic stretching,* a person stretches a muscle to its limit and then makes repetitive bouncing movements. This type of stretch is ineffective and can cause muscle tears and soreness.
- *Static stretching* involves stretching a muscle slowly and gently to its limit, holding it there for a time, then relaxing it (see illustration: Stretching Exercises).
- *Contract-relax stretching* is a variation of static stretching in which pairs of muscles are alternately stretched and relaxed. First one

(a)

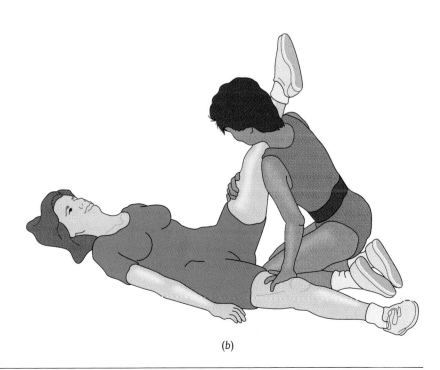

(b)

muscle is contracted against resistance, such as an object or an exercise partner. As that muscle relaxes, the opposing muscle is contracted. Contract-relax stretching is the best way to improve muscle flexibility.

Doing Stretching Exercise   Stretching exercise, even when part of a warm-up routine, should be preceded by a few minutes of activity to increase blood flow and raise muscle temperature. Walking or jogging in place for a few minutes is a good warm-up before stretching. Stretching during the cool-down period helps develop flexibility efficiently because the muscles are warm and can be stretched more.

Begin each exercise by stretching slowly and smoothly until you feel a mild pull. Then hold the stretch for 3 to 30 seconds. (Begin with a short amount of time and increase duration as you progress.) Breathe slowly and deeply, stretching farther while exhaling. Release the muscle, then repeat the stretch several times. You can improve flexibility by performing a routine of stretching exercises three to five times per week. A good stretching session should last 10 to 30 minutes.

Developing a Stretching Program   There are hundreds of different kinds of stretches that can be performed to exercise individual muscles and muscle groups. Exercise and fitness books and magazines can provide instructions on individual exercises. You can develop your own stretching program by selecting sets of exercises that are designed to stretch the muscles you want to use. A runner, for example, would perform exercises that stretch the thighs, calves, Achilles tendon, and torso muscles.

RISK FACTORS
▶ ▶ ▶ ▶ ▶ ▶

Done improperly, stretching exercise can cause injuries. For example, locked-knee toe touches can strain the knees and pull the hamstring muscles in the thigh. The basic rule for stretching is simple: If a movement hurts, stop doing it. (See also AEROBIC DANCE; FITNESS; FITNESS TRAINING; RUNNING.)

SUGAR

Sugar is the smallest and simplest type of CARBOHYDRATE, a NUTRIENT that the body needs in large amounts. The other two types of carbohydrate are STARCH and FIBER. A major source of energy, sugar is an important part of the diet.

In the United States, the average person consumes about 120 pounds (54.5 kg) of sugar a year. Although the body needs sugar, there are good reasons to limit its consumption. Sugar has no VITAMINS or MINERALS and so possesses no nutritional value other than CALORIES. Excessive amounts of sugar are easily converted to *body fat* and can cause *tooth decay*.

The terms for sugar can be recognized by their -*ose* endings: Glucose, fructose, sucrose, galactose, lactose, and maltose are the six sugars found in foods. Depending on its chemical structure, a sugar is classified as either *monosaccharide* or *disaccharide*. A disaccharide is two monosaccharide units linked together.

Differences Among Sugar Foods. *The body needs sugar, but not all foods with sugar are equally nutritious. A can of soda is little more than sugar and water, but an orange has the additional benefits of vitamins, minerals, and fiber.*

Glucose GLUCOSE is a monosaccharide. Also known as blood sugar, it is highly soluble and moves quickly into the bloodstream. Glucose is found in nearly all foods of plant origin.

Fructose Fructose is a monosaccharide and the sweetest of all the sugars. Also called fruit sugar, it is found in fruits and saps. Fructose, unlike glucose, does not need the help of the hormone insulin to enter cells, so it can be used by people with diabetes. A disadvantage of this sugar is that it is more readily converted than are other forms into fat that circulates in the blood.

Sucrose Familiar as table sugar, sucrose is the best known of the three disaccharides. Chemically, it is the union of the monosaccharides glucose and fructose. Its principal sources are sugar cane and sugar beets, and it is also found in a number of fruits, vegetables, and grains. The fructose component of sucrose makes this sugar very sweet, and it is widely used in candy, soft drinks, and baked goods, among many other foods.

Lactose Lactose is a disaccharide that combines glucose and a rarely occurring monosaccharide known as galactose. Lactose is often called milk sugar because it makes up about 5 percent of milk. Babies can easily digest lactose from the moment they are born, which makes milk sugar an excellent source of energy for infants. Some people, however, develop an inability to digest lactose as they grow older, a condition known as *lactose intolerance.*

Honey Like table sugar, honey is a disaccharide made up of glucose and fructose. Contrary to popular opinion, honey is not more nutritious than table sugar—neither possesses vitamins or minerals.

Brown Sugar Brown sugar is made from sugar cane. The process involves turning the sugar cane into a thick, brown syrup known as molasses and then converting the syrup into brown sugar crystals. (See also ARTIFICIAL SWEETENERS; ENERGY, FOOD; FATS, OILS, AND SWEETS GROUP; OVERWEIGHT; DIABETES, **3**.)

▶ SWIMMING

Swimming is an excellent form of AEROBIC EXERCISE. It improves the efficiency of the heart and lungs and uses nearly every muscle group in the body. Swimming rarely causes injuries because the water supporting a swimmer reduces stress on muscles, joints, and bones. All these factors make swimming an ideal FITNESS exercise of special value for people with disabilities as well as those recovering from injuries.

Swimming for Fitness An aerobic swimming workout consists of 30 to 40 minutes of continuous swimming three to four times a week. The best stroke for both burning calories and promoting fitness is the freestyle, or forward crawl. Beginners usually start out with a few laps of a standard pool and gradually add laps until they are swimming 1 to 1.5 miles (about 1.5 to 2.5 km) at each session. In a standard swimming pool, 70 laps equals just under 1 mile.

Swimming takes up to four times as much effort as RUNNING to cover an equal distance, so swimmers need to swim only one-fourth as far to expend the same number of calories as runners do. On the other hand, because swimming is not a *weight-bearing exercise,* it may not strengthen bones or provide the protection against osteoporosis that some other sports may provide.

Convenience and Safety Most swimmers have to locate an indoor pool and travel there to exercise, which may be inconvenient for people with full schedules. In addition, swimmers are prone to dry skin, eye and

Swimming for Fitness. *Swimming is an excellent form of exercise for all types of people.*

sinus irritation, and swimmer's ear, a fungus infection of the ear canal. Goggles, ear plugs, nose clips, and special ear drops can prevent some of these problems. For safety, never swim alone, dive into water unless you know it is deep enough, or swim in excessively cold water. Very cold water can cause *hypothermia,* dangerously low body temperature. (See also EAR INFECTIONS, 2; HYPOTHERMIA, 8.)

UNDERWEIGHT

People who are more than 15 percent below the recommended weight for their height and sex are considered underweight. Eating habits as well as heredity may cause a person to be underweight. In extreme cases of underweight due to an illness or an EATING DISORDER such as anorexia or bulimia, medical help is needed. Otherwise, being slightly underweight does not present a health risk.

To gain weight, try a WEIGHT-GAIN STRATEGY that will help increase the number of calories eaten. Eating larger quantities of healthful foods and sensible snacking during the day should stimulate weight gain in most cases. Moderate exercise may also stimulate the appetite and help the development of muscle. Weight should be gained gradually; about 1 pound (about 0.5 kg) per week is considered safe. (See also WEIGHT ASSESSMENT.)

VEGETABLES

see FRUITS AND VEGETABLES GROUP

VEGETARIAN DIET

A vegetarian diet is one that is made up of vegetables, fruits, grains, nuts, and sometimes animal products like milk and cheese. Vegetarian diets are healthy and nutritious as long as they include a variety of foods that together provide adequate amounts of VITAMINS, MINERALS, PROTEINS, and CALORIES.

Millions of people all over the world are *vegetarians,* or people who eat a vegetarian diet. Some people choose to eat a vegetarian diet for religious, ethical, or health-related reasons. In many developing countries, however, people may eat vegetarian diets of necessity because they cannot afford to raise or buy any meat.

Types of Vegetarians Vegetarians fall into one of four categories. *Vegans* eat only vegetables, fruits, and grains. *Lactovegetarians* add milk products to their diet; *lactoovovegetarians* include both milk products and eggs. *Semivegetarians* eat milk products, eggs, and an occasional serving of fish or poultry.

Eating a Balanced Diet Vegetarians, especially vegans, must be careful to eat a varied, well-balanced diet in adequate amounts. Certain essential NUTRIENTS are much more common in meats, milk products, and

Eating a Vegetarian Diet. *People who eat a vegetarian diet must eat a variety of foods to obtain all the nutrients their bodies need.*

eggs than in foods of plant origin. Vegetarians therefore must adjust their diets to provide all the vitamins, minerals, and protein their bodies need.

One such vitamin is *vitamin B₁₂*, which is found only in animal products such as meat, liver, eggs, and milk. A lack of vitamin B$_{12}$ can cause permanent damage to the brain and nerves and is especially dangerous to developing infants and children. Vegans can obtain vitamin B$_{12}$ by taking a vitamin supplement or by eating foods that have been fortified with vitamin B$_{12}$.

Also lacking in most vegan diets is VITAMIN D, which is found primarily in fish oils, beef, butter, eggs, and milk. This vitamin is essential for normal bone and tooth development. Because plant foods are not a source of vitamin D, vegans must either take a vitamin D supplement or make sure they get regular exposure to the sun, which prompts the body to manufacture its own supplies of the vitamin.

A deficiency of IRON, an important nutrient, may also be a problem for vegetarians. Although present in many vegetables and grains, iron is more easily absorbed from animal products like beef and poultry. Vegetarians who do not eat poultry should eat plant foods high in iron, such as dried beans, spinach, dried fruits, and tofu.

Although many foods of plant origin contain CALCIUM, a vegan diet tends to make the mineral difficult for the body to absorb. Vegans (especially infants and children, who require calcium for healthy development) may need supplements or a soy "milk" fortified with calcium as a part of their diet.

HEALTHY CHOICES

All vegetarians must ensure that they eat an adequate amount of protein. This may be especially difficult for vegans, because plant proteins are of lower quality than are those of fish, poultry, beef, and milk products. Plant proteins from individual food sources are incomplete; none contain all of the essential *amino acids*. As a result, vegans need to consume proteins from different plant sources in order to supply themselves with complete proteins. A common way to do so is to combine grains with legumes, such as rice with beans or bread with peanut butter.

Benefits of a Vegetarian Diet When adequate in amount and variety, vegetarian diets offer significant health benefits. Low in FATS and high in FIBER, they lower the likelihood of colon cancer and diverticulitis and aid in weight loss and the prevention of OBESITY. Studies have shown that a low-fat vegetarian diet reduces the risks of heart disease and diabetes. In addition, vegan diets are free of CHOLESTEROL and low in saturated fats (which serves to lower blood cholesterol levels) and low in SODIUM and high in POTASSIUM (which reduces the risk of developing hypertension). (See also DIETS; VITAMIN B COMPLEX.)

▶ VITAMIN A

Vitamin A is an organic chemical substance essential for normal growth and the development of strong bones and teeth. Also called *retinol*, it promotes healthy cell structure in the skin and linings of the respiratory, digestive, and urinary tracts, which protect these systems from infection. Vitamin A also promotes normal vision.

Prescription medications have recently been developed from vitamin A. These medications are applied directly to the skin to treat acne and damage to the skin from too much sun exposure.

RISK FACTORS
▶ ▶ ▶ ▶ ▶ ▶

Vitamin A Deficiency A deficiency of vitamin A is rare in a developed country like the United States, but it can result from vitamin absorption problems in the intestine or long-term treatment with certain drugs. Poor diets in developing countries, however, result in vitamin A deficiencies in many children. Symptoms of deficiency include dry, inflamed eyes, poor night vision, or blindness; dry, rough skin; loss of appetite; diarrhea; lowered resistance to infection; and, in severe cases, weak bones and teeth.

Sampling of Foods Rich in Vitamin A. *The recommended dietary allowance for vitamin A is 1,000 mcg for men and 800 mcg for women. Foods rich in this vitamin include beef liver, carrots, and winter squash.*

Recommended Intake of Vitamin A   Vitamin A is a *fat-soluble vitamin*. The RECOMMENDED DIETARY ALLOWANCE (RDA) for vitamin A is 1,000 mcg for men and 800 mcg for women. It is stored in the body's liver and fatty tissue, which can hold up to a year's supply. Excessive amounts can build up, resulting in symptoms such as headache, tiredness, nausea, loss of appetite, diarrhea, weight loss, dry and itchy skin, and hair loss. In women, too much vitamin A can cause irregular menstrual periods and, during pregnancy, birth defects. Extreme cases of excess vitamin A may cause swollen feet and ankles, bone pain, and enlargement of the liver and spleen.

HEALTHY CHOICES
●●●●●●●●●●●●

Sources of Vitamin A   Rich sources of vitamin A include liver, fish-liver oils, egg yolk, milk and dairy products, and margarine. Many fruits and vegetables contain BETA CAROTENE, which is readily converted to vitamin A in the body. Good sources of beta carotene include carrots, sweet potatoes, winter squash, kale, broccoli, spinach, apricots, and peaches. (See also VITAMINS.)

▶ **VITAMIN B COMPLEX**   Vitamin B complex is a group of water-soluble vitamins that includes *thiamine* (vitamin B_1), *riboflavin* (B_2), *niacin, pantothenic acid, pyridoxine* (B_6), *biotin, folic acid,* and *vitamin B_{12}*. As a group, these vitamins are essential for energy metabolism and health maintenance. Each component of this complex of vitamins is important to good health. Harmful effects from excess doses of B vitamins are rare because the body normally excretes what it does not use.

Thiamine   Thiamine aids enzymes (substances that produce chemical reactions) in breaking down and using carbohydrates. It also helps the nerves, muscles, and heart to function efficiently. A mild deficiency causes tiredness, irritability, loss of appetite, and sleeping problems. A severe deficiency can cause beriberi (a disease affecting the nerves in the legs), abdominal pain, depression, constipation, and impaired memory. Elderly people who eat a poor diet, people with extremely high energy

RISK FACTORS
▶ ▶ ▶ ▶ ▶ ▶

FOODS RICH IN B-COMPLEX VITAMINS	
Vitamin	**Foods**
Thiamine	Whole-grain breads and cereals, wheat germ, bran, brown rice, pasta, legumes, eggs, fish, pork, liver
Riboflavin	Liver, milk, eggs, cheese, whole-grain and enriched breads and cereals, brewer's yeast, leafy green vegetables
Niacin	Liver, lean meat, poultry, fish, whole grains, nuts, dried beans
Pantothenic acid, pyridoxine, biotin	Meats, fish, whole grains, wheat germ, potatoes, dried beans, fruits, vegetables
Folic acid, vitamin B_{12}	Eggs, liver, milk, leafy green vegetables

requirements, or people with overactive thyroid glands may experience thiamine deficiency. For most people, however, a varied diet provides enough of this vitamin. The RECOMMENDED DIETARY ALLOWANCE (RDA) for thiamine is 1.4 mg for men and 1.1 mg for women.

Riboflavin   Riboflavin aids enzymes that break down carbohydrates, fats, and proteins and convert them to energy. A deficiency may cause chapped lips, soreness in and around the mouth, and eye disorders. The RDA for riboflavin is 1.2 mg.

Niacin   Niacin helps enzymes break down carbohydrates and fats, maintains nervous and digestive systems, produces sex hormones, and promotes healthy skin. Niacin in large doses is sometimes prescribed by doctors to treat high blood cholesterol levels. A deficiency can cause sore and cracked skin, mouth and tongue inflammation, and mental disturbances. The RDA for niacin is 16 to 19 mg for men and 13 to 14 mg for women.

RISK FACTORS
▶ ▶ ▶ ▶ ▶ ▶

Pantothenic Acid, Pyridoxine (B₆), and Biotin   These vitamins aid enzymes that break down carbohydrates, fats, and proteins. Deficiencies among people who eat a varied diet are rare. Extremely high amounts of pyridoxine are believed to cause a problem with the nervous system called neuritis.

Folic Acid and Vitamin B₁₂   Vitamin B_{12} and folic acid work together to produce DNA—the part of the cell that stores the body's hereditary characteristics. Recent research suggests that folic-acid supplements may help prevent certain birth defects including spina bifida and anencephaly as well as cervical cancer. A deficiency of either vitamin produces *anemia,* a deficiency of red blood cells. (See also VITAMINS; ANEMIA, **3.**)

RISK FACTORS
▶ ▶ ▶ ▶ ▶ ▶

▶ **VITAMIN C**

Vitamin C is an organic chemical substance that performs several important functions. Also called *ascorbic acid,* it works with enzymes (substances that spark chemical reactions in the body) to develop and maintain healthy bones, teeth, gums, ligaments, and blood vessels. Vitamin C helps produce chemicals that transmit nerve impulses and adrenal gland hormones. It also helps the body heal its wounds and absorb iron from the digestive tract.

Recent studies have suggested that vitamin C may play a role in preventing cancer, slowing the development of heart disease, and helping the immune system fight infection. This may be due to the vitamin's *antioxidant* properties. Vitamins that are antioxidants are able to fight certain chemical substances called *free radicals* that damage cells, opening the door for disease and the effects of aging. (See also VITAMIN E.)

RISK FACTORS
▶ ▶ ▶ ▶ ▶ ▶

Vitamin C Deficiency   A mild deficiency of vitamin C can cause swollen gums, nosebleeds, and general aches and pains. Severe deficiency can lead to *anemia,* a deficiency of red blood cells, or *scurvy,* a rare, potentially fatal, disease.

Sampling of Foods Rich in Vitamin C. *The recommended dietary allowance for vitamin C is 60 mg per day. Foods rich in this vitamin include oranges, broccoli, and cantaloupe.*

Recommended Intake of Vitamin C Vitamin C is a *water-soluble vitamin*, which means that it cannot be stored in large amounts in the body. A regular supply must be included in the diet. The RECOMMENDED DIETARY ALLOWANCE (RDA) for vitamin C is 60 mg, an amount usually included in a balanced diet. One popular theory suggests that very high doses of vitamin C can prevent colds, but the evidence is inconclusive. Furthermore, large doses can cause nausea, stomach cramps, diarrhea, and kidney stones.

HEALTHY CHOICES

Sources of Vitamin C Vitamin C is found in fresh fruits and vegetables. Citrus fruits, tomatoes, leafy green vegetables, potatoes, green peppers, strawberries, and cantaloupe are excellent sources. Vitamin C is more effective when accompanied by *bioflavonoids*, substances that occur naturally in fruits and vegetables and complement vitamin C. Foods rich in both elements include citrus fruits, cherries, rose hips, sweet and hot peppers, spinach, and other dark-green leafy vegetables. (See also VITAMINS; ANEMIA, 3.)

▶ VITAMIN D

Vitamin D is a group of related organic chemical substances that maintains strong bones and teeth by controlling the body's use of calcium and phosphorus. It helps regulate levels of calcium and phosphate in the bones and blood and stimulates the kidneys to retain calcium. Vitamin D is present in many foods and is also produced by the body when the skin is exposed to sunlight. Vitamin D is a *fat-soluble vitamin* that is stored in the body's fatty tissue and the liver.

RISK FACTORS
▶ ▶ ▶ ▶ ▶ ▶

Recommended Intake of Vitamin D Both too little and too much vitamin D can cause medical problems. The RECOMMENDED DIETARY ALLOWANCE (RDA) for vitamin D is 5 to 10 mcg for adults and 10 mcg for children. An excess of vitamin D in the body is rarely a result of eating too many foods with high levels of the vitamin. Taking large doses of

Sampling of Foods Rich in Vitamin D. *The recommended dietary allowance for vitamin D is 5 to 10 mcg per day. Foods rich in this vitamin include eggs, liver, fortified milk, tuna, salmon, and sardines.*

vitamin D supplements, however, can cause weakness, abnormal thirst, increased urination, gastrointestinal disturbances, and depression. Because vitamin D is fat soluble, excessive intake over a long period can cause calcium deposits in the kidneys and hardening of the blood-vessel walls.

RISK FACTORS
▶ ▶ ▶ ▶ ▶ ▶

Vitamin D Deficiency Vitamin D deficiency can lead to a softening of the bones. In children this condition is called *rickets,* and in adults, it is called *osteomalacia.* Deficiencies are rare but can occur among people who eat a poor diet; individuals with a disorder that prevents the intestine from absorbing the vitamin; and people who are deprived of sunlight, such as night workers.

Sources of Vitamin D Fortified milk and other dairy products, oily fish, liver, and egg yolks are rich sources of vitamin D. (See also VITAMINS.)

▶ VITAMIN E

Vitamin E is a group of organic chemical substances that performs a number of vital functions. It is essential for creating and sustaining normal cell structure, forming red blood cells, and maintaining the activity of enzymes (substances that promote chemical reactions in the body). In addition, vitamin E is an *antioxidant,* which means it is able to fight certain molecules called *free radicals* that damage red blood cells and lung tissue, opening the door for disease. A lack of vitamin E leads to destruction of red blood cells and *anemia.* Vitamin E deficiency is rare and is usually caused by intestinal absorption problems or liver disorders.

Vitamin E is a *fat-soluble vitamin,* which means that it is stored for long periods in the liver and fatty tissues. The RECOMMENDED DIETARY ALLOWANCE (RDA) for vitamin E is 8 to 10 mg for adults. Excessive intake of vitamin E may cause abdominal pain, nausea, and diarrhea.

Sampling of Foods Rich in Vitamin E. *The recommended dietary allowance for vitamin E is 8 to 10 mg per day. Foods rich in this vitamin include many fruits and vegetables and vegetable oils, such as margarine, salad dressing, shortening, soybean oils, and wheat-germ oil.*

A balanced diet provides adequate amounts of vitamin E, which is found in large amounts in vegetable oils, nuts, meat, leafy green vegetables, cereals, wheat germ, and egg yolks. (See also VITAMIN C; VITAMINS.)

▶ VITAMIN K

Vitamin K is a group of organic chemical substances essential for blood clotting. A *fat-soluble vitamin*, vitamin K is stored in the body's liver and fatty tissues. Rich sources of vitamin K include leafy green vegetables, cauliflower, vegetable oils, egg yolks, cheese, pork, and liver. A deficiency of vitamin K reduces the blood's ability to clot and may result in abnormal bleeding from the nose, gums, intestines, or urinary tract.

RISK FACTORS
▶ ▶ ▶ ▶ ▶ ▶

Sampling of Foods Rich in Vitamin K. *The recommended dietary allowance for vitamin K is 70 to 140 mg for adults. Foods rich in this vitamin include spinach, kale, milk, pork, and liver.*

Deficiencies of vitamin K are rare because it is readily available in the diet and is also produced by intestinal bacteria. Supplements of vitamin K are given to newborns, however, because they do not have enough intestinal bacteria to produce vitamin K until they are about 2 weeks old.

The RECOMMENDED DIETARY ALLOWANCE (RDA) of vitamin K is 70 to 140 mg for adults. Daily intake above this level has no known harmful effects. (See also VITAMINS.)

▶ ## VITAMINS

Vitamins are organic chemical substances that trigger a wide variety of bodily processes. Essential for human health, they are required in very small amounts that are generally supplied by a balanced diet. A few are manufactured by the body itself. The 13 known vitamins are A, C, D, E, K, and the 8 B-complex vitamins.

RECOMMENDED DIETARY ALLOWANCES OF VITAMINS

Category (age, sex, or condition)	Fat-soluble vitamins				Water-soluble vitamins								
	Vita-min A (*)	Vita-min D (mcg)	Vita-min E (mg)	Vita-min K (mcg)	Vita-min C (mg)	Thia-mine (mg)	Ribo-flavin (mg)	Nia-cin (**)	Vita-min B₆ (mg)	Folic acid (mcg)	Vita-min B₁₂ (mcg)	Bio-tin (mcg)†	Panto-thenic acid (mg)†
Infants													
0–½	375	7.5	3	5	30	0.3	0.4	5	0.3	25	0.3	10	2
½–1	375	10.0	4	10	35	0.4	0.5	6	0.6	35	0.5	15	3
Children													
1–3	400	10.0	6	15	40	0.7	0.8	9	1.0	50	0.7	20	3
4–6	500	10.0	7	20	45	0.9	1.1	12	1.1	75	1.0	25	3–4
7–10	700	10.0	7	30	45	1.0	1.2	13	1.4	100	1.4	30	4–5
Males													
11–14	1,000	10.0	10	45	50	1.3	1.5	17	1.7	150	2.0	30–100	4–7
15–18	1,000	10.0	10	65	60	1.5	1.8	20	2.0	200	2.0	30–100	4–7
19–24	1,000	10.0	10	70	60	1.5	1.7	19	2.0	200	2.0	30–100	4–7
25–50	1,000	5.0	10	80	60	1.5	1.7	19	2.0	200	2.0	30–100	4–7
51+	1,000	5.0	10	80	60	1.2	1.4	15	2.0	200	2.0	30–100	4–7
Females													
11–14	800	10.0	8	45	50	1.1	1.3	15	1.4	150	2.0	30–100	4–7
15–18	800	10.0	8	55	60	1.1	1.3	15	1.5	180	2.0	30–100	4–7
19–24	800	10.0	8	60	60	1.1	1.3	15	1.6	180	2.0	30–100	4–7
25–50	800	5.0	8	65	60	1.1	1.3	15	1.6	180	2.0	30–100	4–7
51+	800	5.0	8	65	60	1.0	1.2	13	1.6	180	2.0	30–100	4–7
Pregnant females	800	10.0	10	65	70	1.5	1.6	17	2.2	400	2.2	30–100	4–7
Lactating females													
1st 6 months	1,300	10.0	12	65	95	1.6	1.8	20	2.1	280	2.6	30–100	4–7
2nd 6 months	1,200	10.0	11	65	90	1.6	1.7	20	2.1	260	2.6	30–100	4–7

*Mcg RE (retinol equivalent). 1 RE is equal to 1 mcg of retinol or 6 mcg of beta carotene.

** Mg NE (niacin equivalent). 1 NE is equal to 1 mg of niacin or 60 mg of dietary tryptophan.

† Information for these vitamins is provided as estimated safe and adequate daily intakes, rather than as recommended allowances.

Adapted with permission from *Recommended Dietary Allowances,* 10th edition. Copyright 1989 by the National Academy of Sciences. Published by the National Academy Press, Washington, D.C.

Vitamins are divided into two groups: fat-soluble vitamins (A, D, E, and K) and water-soluble vitamins (C and B-complex vitamins). *Fat-soluble vitamins* are stored in the body's liver and fatty tissues. *Water-soluble vitamins* are stored in the body for only a short time, and any excess passes out of the body in the urine.

The U.S. RECOMMENDED DIETARY ALLOWANCES (RDAs) provide guidelines for meeting daily vitamin needs and avoiding deficiency or toxicity (see chart: Recommended Dietary Allowances of Vitamins). A healthful, varied diet usually provides all the vitamins people need. Vitamin deficiency, therefore, is rare in the United States. Certain circumstances, however, can increase the body's need for vitamins, such as some illnesses, pregnancy, and breast-feeding. In these cases a doctor may prescribe vitamin supplements.

Recent research suggests that ingesting certain vitamins in doses above the RDA guidelines can prevent some birth defects and diseases, including heart disease and cancer, as well as protect against some effects of aging, such as cataracts. But many medical experts believe the information is too new to use in making recommendations to the public. In particular, questions involving the vitamin amounts and the form in which they should be ingested are unresolved. "Megadoses" are known to cause a dangerous excess of some vitamins in body tissues. An excess of fat-soluble vitamins is especially harmful. These vitamins build up in the fatty tissues in the body and can reach toxic levels. Traditional medical opinion holds that taking vitamin supplements in doses within the RDA guidelines has no negative health effects but no significant health benefits other than to prevent deficiency diseases such as rickets. (See also VITAMIN A; VITAMIN B COMPLEX; VITAMIN C; VITAMIN D; VITAMIN E; VITAMIN K.)

► WALKING

Walking is a good exercise to strengthen the heart and lungs, improve overall FITNESS, and maintain or reduce weight. People of any age and virtually any fitness level can walk for exercise. It can be done year-round and requires no special equipment except for a pair of comfortable walking shoes.

Benefits of Walking   Walking for exercise has many benefits. In addition to strengthening the heart and lungs, it helps reduce blood pressure and CHOLESTEROL levels in the blood. It tones and strengthens muscles and improves circulation. Because walking is a weight-bearing exercise, it also strengthens some bones and reduces the risk of developing osteoporosis later in life, a disease that causes bones to become brittle and more prone to fracture, especially in women.

Walking is an AEROBIC EXERCISE like RUNNING, SWIMMING, and CYCLING. It elevates the HEART RATE and increases the ability of the body to use oxygen. Walking burns almost as many calories as the calories burned in running the same distance, but it requires less effort and causes fewer injuries. A 160-pound (about 72-kg) person who walks briskly—at a rate of about 3.5 miles (about 6 km) per hour—for 30 minutes can burn more than 150 calories.

Walking for Fitness. *Walking alone or with a friend can be a very pleasant form of exercise.*

How It Is Done   Walking for exercise is different from casual walking or strolling. To walk for exercise, walk in a smooth, steady rhythm as you swing your arms briskly. With each step, land on your heel and push off with the toe. Carrying hand weights of up to 3 pounds (about 1 kg) gives the upper body a workout and increases the aerobic effects.

To begin a walking program, start out by walking three times a week for 20 to 25 minutes. Gradually increase the pace and frequency of your walks until you can walk briskly for 30 to 60 minutes five times a week. Some people walk measured miles while others walk for specific lengths of time. The most important part of any program is that it be a regular part of a weekly routine.

Walking Safety   Walking seldom causes injuries, but out-of-shape walkers may experience soreness in the hips and shins. Warm-up exercises that stretch and flex the hip and leg muscles can reduce soreness. Do not stop walking abruptly; go through a cool-down period to prevent your muscles from tightening. Wear loose, comfortable clothing and dress warmly in winter to avoid losing body heat. Many shopping malls have walking programs that allow people to exercise safely in any kind of weather. (See also ATHLETIC FOOTWEAR; ENDURANCE.)

▶ WATER

Water is the most abundant substance in the human body, accounting for 55 to 70 percent of the average adult's weight. Although it strictly has no nutritional value, water is present in and vital to the operation of every living cell and tissue.

Water is essential to life: Without it, humans can survive for only a matter of days. For that reason, the body maintains a careful balance between water consumed (in foods and beverages) and water lost (through urination, perspiration, and respiration).

Functions of Water   One of the chief functions of water in the body is to carry dissolved NUTRIENTS to the cells. This is done by both the *blood* and the *lymph* (a fluid that bathes all soft tissue); both consist largely of water. These fluids also carry away the cells' waste products. The *kidneys* then filter out these wastes and pass them out of the body in the form of *urine*, which is also composed largely of water.

Water has a number of additional functions in the body. Among them is its role in helping to physically break down foods to aid in DIGESTION. It also acts as a *catalyst* in many chemical reactions in the body. Water in the form of PERSPIRATION cools the body through the process of evaporation. Water is also the main ingredient of body fluids that cushion and protect vital organs, including the brain and various organs in the abdomen.

HEALTHY CHOICES
■ ● ● ● ● ● ● ● ● ● ● ●

Water in the Diet   Most water in the diet comes from BEVERAGES such as tap water, coffee, tea, milk, fruit juices, and soft drinks. Most healthy individuals should drink the equivalent of six to eight glasses of water a day. The remainder of the body's requirement of water comes from solid foods. Fruits and vegetables have a particularly high water content (see illustration: Foods with High Water Content).

Foods with High Water Content. *A third of the recommended daily intake of water can come from foods. Foods high in water include lettuce (96 percent water), asparagus (92 percent), oranges (86 percent), and potatoes (80 percent).*

Maintaining a Balance   An adequate level of water in the body—the body's water balance—is maintained by the activities of the kidneys and by changes in *thirst* sensations and fluid intake. When fluid intake is high, the body excretes large quantities of urine. When fluid intake is low, less urine is produced, and more water is absorbed in the blood.

The thirst sensation is triggered by a complex biochemical process when the body needs more water. Thirst makes a person feel a physical need to consume fluids. Food substances such as SUGAR and SALT, which require water to be dissolved, also tend to make a person thirsty. The thirst sensation, however, is often a poor guide for adequate fluid intake. People who exercise strenuously or who work in hot climates should drink even when they are not thirsty.

RISK FACTORS
▶ ▶ ▶ ▶ ▶ ▶

Too little water in the body can lead to a potentially life-threatening medical condition called DEHYDRATION. This can result from inadequate water intake, excessive water loss, or a combination of the two. Common causes of dehydration include excessive perspiration due to hot weather or extreme exertion as well as *diarrhea* and *vomiting*.

In some medical disorders, such as kidney or heart disease, the body cannot excrete excess water adequately. This leads to an accumulation of fluids in the body tissues, a swelling condition called *edema*. (See also BODY METABOLISM; MINERALS; DIURETIC, 7.)

▶ **WEIGHT ASSESSMENT**   Weight assessment is the process of analyzing a person's weight and body composition. BODY COMPOSITION is the ratio of body fat to bone and muscle. Information about weight and body composition can tell you whether you are UNDERWEIGHT, of normal weight, OVERWEIGHT, or obese. Even if your weight is appropriate, the information about body composition can provide one measure of overall FITNESS. Weight assessment can be used to plan a diet and exercise program and to help develop an accurate *body image*. (See also OBESITY.)

SUGGESTED WEIGHTS FOR ADULTS

Dietary Guidelines for Americans, 1990			Metropolitan Life Insurance Company Guidelines, 1959		
Height without shoes	**Weight without clothes (lb)**		**Height without shoes**	**Weight without clothes (lb)***	
	Ages 19–34	**35 and over**		**Men**	**Women**
5 ft	97–128	108–138	4 ft 10 in		92–121
5 ft 1 in	101–132	111–143	4 ft 11 in		95–124
5 ft 2 in	104–137	115–148	5 ft		98–127
5 ft 3 in	107–141	119–152	5 ft 1 in	105–134	101–130
5 ft 4 in	111–146	122–157	5 ft 2 in	108–137	104–134
5 ft 5 in	114–150	126–162	5 ft 3 in	111–141	107–138
5 ft 6 in	118–155	130–167	5 ft 4 in	114–145	110–142
5 ft 7 in	121–160	134–172	5 ft 5 in	117–149	114–146
5 ft 8 in	125–164	138–178	5 ft 6 in	121–154	118–150
5 ft 9 in	129–169	142–183	5 ft 7 in	125–159	122–154
5 ft 10 in	132–174	146–188	5 ft 8 in	129–163	126–159
5 ft 11 in	136–179	151–194	5 ft 9 in	133–167	130–164
6 ft	140–184	155–199	5 ft 10 in	137–172	134–169
6 ft 1 in	144–189	159–205	5 ft 11 in	141–177	
6 ft 2 in	148–195	164–210	6 ft	145–182	
6 ft 3 in	152–200	168–216	6 ft 1 in	149–187	
6 ft 4 in	156–205	173–222	6 ft 2 in	153–192	
6 ft 5 in	160–211	177–228	6 ft 3 in	157–197	
6 ft 6 in	164–216	182–234			

*For women 18–25 years, subtract 1 pound for each year under 25.

Source: Adapted from the 1959 Metropolitan Desirable Weight Table.

Suggested Weights for Adults. *The guidelines for suggested weights for adults were revised in 1990 to reflect research indicating that it is normal and not unhealthy for people to gain a little weight as they grow older. The new chart is controversial, however, because it does not have different categories for men and women.*

There are several methods of weight assessment. Some methods compare a person's weight with average weights for men or women of the same height. Other methods specifically measure body fat to determine body composition. This is useful because two people of the same height and weight can have different proportions of body fat. One may be unfit and need to lose some fat, whereas the other's weight is largely made up of muscle, an indication of fitness.

Height and Weight Chart The simplest tool for learning about a person's weight is a height and weight chart (see chart: Suggested Weights for Adults). Such charts show a range of average weights for each height. People who weigh more than 10 percent above their recommended weight for their height are considered overweight; people more than 20 percent over their recommended weight are considered obese. The advantages of using a chart are its convenience and the ready comparison with averages that it provides.

Body-Mass Index The body-mass index (BMI) uses height and weight data in a different way. The BMI is a ratio in which weight (in kilograms) is divided by height (in meters) squared. The ratio is used by health professionals to estimate body fat. A BMI over 27 causes concern about excess weight (see graph: Body-Mass Index).

Fatfold Measurement A fatfold (or skinfold) measurement gauges the fat under the skin. An instrument called a caliper is used to measure the thickness of a fold of skin on the back of the upper arm, the shoulder blade, the thigh, or other areas (see illustration: Fatfold Measurement). The measurements are used to estimate body fat. The accuracy of this method depends on the precise use of the caliper.

Hydrostatic Weighing Hydrostatic (or underwater) weighing is another method of measuring body fat. Because muscle and bone are heavier and more dense than fat, fat causes the body to float in water. Hydrostatic weighing involves first weighing a person on a regular scale.

Body-Mass Index. *To estimate your body-mass index, place one end of a ruler on the chart at your weight without clothes and the other end at your height without shoes. The point at which the ruler intersects the middle scale shows your BMI.*

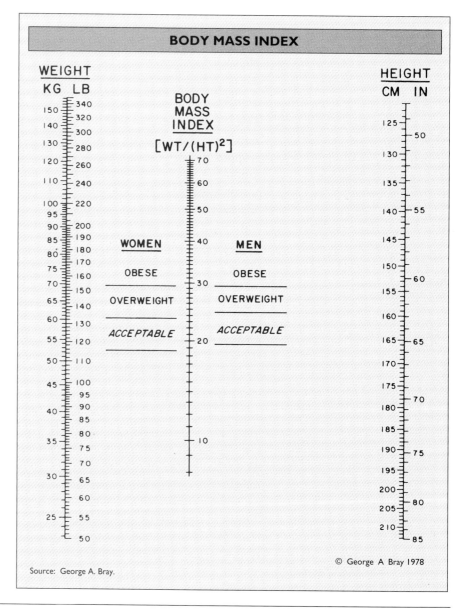

BODY MASS INDEX

Source: George A. Bray.

© George A Bray 1978

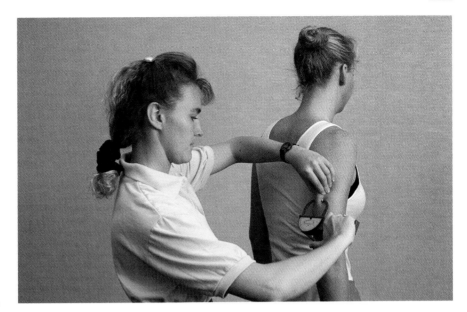

Fatfold Measurement. *To take a fatfold measurement, a professional uses a caliper to measure the amount of fat in a fold of skin at one or more points on the body. Skill in using the caliper is essential for an accurate measurement.*

Then the person is weighed again while he or she is completely submerged in water. The two weight measurements are compared to calculate the amount of fat and lean tissue. This method of weight assessment can be quite accurate; however, it is relatively expensive, and some people dislike being under water.

Electric Conductivity   The electric conductivity method (also called bioelectrical impedance) uses the body's water content to estimate the proportion of fat. Lean tissue contains water, but fat does not. Water will conduct an electric current. In this method, electrodes are attached to a person's wrist and ankles and a weak electric current is sent through the body. A computer notes how much of the current is lost; from this information the percentage of body fat can be estimated.

Waist-to-Hip Ratio   A good self-method for estimating the proportion of body fat is the waist-to-hip ratio. This is determined by dividing waist measurement (at the navel) by hip measurement (at the hipbone). For women, the result should be 0.8 or less; for men, 1.0 or less. This method is particularly useful because it measures abdominal fat, which is a greater RISK FACTOR for health problems than is fat lower in the body. However, this method may not be as accurate as the skinfold, hydrostatic, and electric conductivity tests for determining body composition.

Uses of Weight-Assessment Data   Choosing a method of weight assessment in any particular situation depends on the intended purpose. Some methods are more convenient; others are complex but more precise. Because a person's mental image of his or her body is often inaccurate, it can be helpful to have an objective assessment before setting weight-change goals. Accurate information about body composition can also help people to learn about their bodies and to focus on those areas that need change. People who are tempted to diet sometimes discover that their weight falls within the normal range for their height. Careful weight assessment can save some people the trouble of unnecessary diets and help others to choose the best approach to meet their needs. (See also DIETS; EATING DISORDERS; WEIGHT-GAIN STRATEGY; WEIGHT-LOSS STRATEGY.)

HEALTHY CHOICES

▶ WEIGHT-GAIN STRATEGY

A weight-gain strategy is a change in eating habits designed to increase a person's weight. Some people find it difficult to gain weight; they tend to burn off all the calories they take in. Following a strategy can help those who are chronically UNDERWEIGHT to eat more and to make sure that their extra calories produce a weight gain.

Two changes in eating habits are essential to any weight-gain strategy: increasing the proportion of high-calorie foods in the diet and simply eating larger quantities of food. Moderate exercise will help convert gained pounds into muscle as well as fat.

Consuming More Calories If you need to increase your CALORIE intake, try to eat more high-calorie foods at meals. This, of course, is the opposite of the advice given to people who are trying to maintain their weight or lose weight. One way is to add some extra FATS to your foods; by weight, fats have more calories than do either CARBOHYDRATES or PROTEINS. Put some butter on your vegetables or sour cream on a potato. To gain 1 pound (0.5 kg) per week, you will need to add at least 500 calories per day to your diet. Use a calorie chart to identify high-calorie foods that you find appealing.

Changing Eating Habits A change in the way you eat is also necessary if you are to become able to consume larger quantities. Try not to fill up on soups, beverages, or salads early in a meal. Instead, eat high-calorie foods first. Eat snacks between meals, but not so close to mealtime that they ruin your appetite for full-size meals. A high-calorie snack at bedtime can help.

CONSULT A
PHYSICIAN

Cautions Anyone who has lost weight unexpectedly should consult a physician to be sure the weight loss is not a symptom of a health problem that needs treatment. For people who have always been thin, gaining weight is usually more a matter of choice than of necessity. Being a few pounds underweight poses no health problems and, from a health standpoint, is preferable to being overweight. Still, many thin people would rather gain a few pounds, usually because they think doing so would improve their appearance.

HEALTHY CHOICES
●●●●●●●●●●●

If you try a weight-gain strategy, be careful about adding fats to your diet. Too much fat is bad for anyone. The added fats should be balanced with extra carbohydrates found in foods such as potatoes, rice, pasta, and bread. The best weight-gain strategy uses nutritious foods to produce a slow, steady gain until the desired goal is reached. (See also BODY METABOLISM; FATS, OILS, AND SWEETS GROUP; WEIGHT ASSESSMENT; WEIGHT MANAGEMENT.)

▶ WEIGHT-LOSS STRATEGY

A weight-loss strategy is a change in lifestyle for the purpose of losing excess body fat. Weight-loss strategies are usually used by people who are OVERWEIGHT or obese. An important reason to lose weight is to decrease the many health risks associated with excess weight. Another frequent motivation is to improve one's physical appearance. (See also OBESITY.)

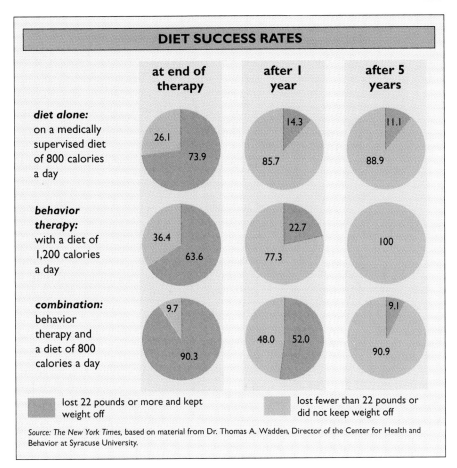

DIET SUCCESS RATES

	at end of therapy	after 1 year	after 5 years
diet alone: on a medically supervised diet of 800 calories a day	26.1 / 73.9	14.3 / 85.7	11.1 / 88.9
behavior therapy: with a diet of 1,200 calories a day	36.4 / 63.6	22.7 / 77.3	100
combination: behavior therapy and a diet of 800 calories a day	9.7 / 90.3	48.0 / 52.0	9.1 / 90.9

■ lost 22 pounds or more and kept weight off   ■ lost fewer than 22 pounds or did not keep weight off

Source: The New York Times, based on material from Dr. Thomas A. Wadden, Director of the Center for Health and Behavior at Syracuse University.

Diet Success Rates. *A panel convened by the National Institutes of Health in 1992 studied group weight-loss programs as well as other types of commercial programs and products. The panel found that long-term success rates are very low and recommended that anyone considering starting a diet "examine the scientific data" on safety and effectiveness.*

Weight-loss strategies vary, depending on individual needs. Some are meant to be used for a short time in order to reach a goal. Others call for a permanent change in eating habits. Some involve a minor reduction in food, whereas others offer a comprehensive plan of DIET and EXERCISE. Because there are so many choices, it helps to know what makes a weight-loss strategy effective.

Elements of an Effective Strategy The main component of any weight-loss strategy is usually a change in diet. In order to lose weight, a person should eat fewer CALORIES each day than the body will burn for energy. One pound (0.5 kg) of body fat tissue results from about 3,500 excess calories. Eating 500 fewer calories every day, therefore, will produce a loss of 1 pound per week. Weight loss tends to be faster at the beginning of a diet, because a lot of water—not fat—is lost. Then the rate slows somewhat. In general, high-calorie foods, especially those of the FATS, OILS, AND SWEETS GROUP, should be avoided, and nutritional low-calorie foods should replace them.

Exercise can also significantly aid weight loss. Raising your level of activity causes you to burn more calories. AEROBIC EXERCISE (brisk walking, jogging, cycling) is most effective. A combination of diet and exercise is usually suggested as the best way to lose excess weight. Regular exercise is particularly valuable as a way to maintain weight loss.

A change in eating habits may be needed in order for a weight-loss strategy to work well. A person who is overweight may have developed habits of overeating, or eating too many of the wrong kinds of foods. Breaking these habits can help the person avoid regaining lost pounds. Problem eating habits vary, but helpful changes in behavior include eating more slowly, taking smaller portions of food, avoiding shopping for food when hungry, eating regular meals, and not skipping meals.

CONSULT A PHYSICIAN

Medical professionals can offer useful advice about losing weight. They can help with the decision about whether or not to lose weight and, if so, how much, and they can help with the choice of an effective strategy. They can also offer advice on whether a particular weight-loss program is safe and healthy.

There are many health benefits to be gained by losing extra pounds. Excess weight has been shown to increase the risks of diseases such as diabetes, high blood pressure, and heart disease. Lowering the risk for these diseases can help people live longer and improve the quality of their lives.

Group weight-loss programs, such as Weight Watchers, are one popular way of dieting. These groups offer support that many people find useful. The programs often provide information about nutrition. Most also use comprehensive plans that combine diet and exercise to help people achieve their goals. The long-term success rates of group programs as well as other types of commercial programs and products are very low, however.

Weight-Loss Strategies to Avoid   Most nutritionists do not recommend losing excess weight too quickly. Doing so can cause health problems; in addition, weight lost quickly is often regained. There are many FAD DIETS that appeal to the desire for a quick fix. Even when nutritionally sound, their long-term results are often disappointing. It is a good idea to get medical advice before trying any diet that severely restricts the number of daily calories.

A steady pattern of losing and regaining pounds (sometimes called yo-yo dieting) may also be hazardous. Experts suggest that a gradual loss of 1 or 2 pounds (0.5 to 1 kg) per week is safer and more effective than sudden loss or repeated dieting.

Some people feel social pressure to lose weight. People may attempt to lose weight when they are not actually overweight, which can cause serious health problems. (See also EATING DISORDERS.)

HEALTHY CHOICES

Healthful Weight Loss   The best weight-loss strategy is one that will enable you to achieve and maintain a normal weight. A gradual weight loss resulting from a nutritious diet, good eating habits, and exercise is usually most successful. If you feel you need to lose weight, first determine your goals. Then select a strategy that is safe, effective, and long-lasting to get the most satisfying results. (See also DIET AIDS; DIET FOOD; WEIGHT ASSESSMENT; WEIGHT MANAGEMENT.)

▶ **WEIGHT MANAGEMENT**   Weight management is the following of a diet and exercise program to maintain ideal body weight. Successful weight management is achieved by combining proper NUTRITION with sensible eating and exercise habits. For weight management to be effective, it must be part of a person's LIFESTYLE.

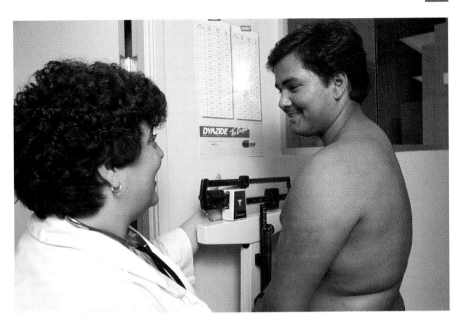

Weight Management. *The most significant goal of weight management is to manage weight with an eye to body composition.*

An important part of weight management involves managing BODY COMPOSITION, particularly the amount of fat in the body. The percentage of fat in a person's body affects his or her physical and social health. Being OVERWEIGHT or UNDERWEIGHT can reduce the body's stamina and may increase risk for diseases such as heart disease and hypertension. In addition, a person's weight affects his or her self-image, self-esteem, and relationships with others.

How the Body Regulates Weight   The body maintains its weight when the amount of *food energy* taken in as CALORIES equals the amount of *physical energy* expended in calories. When intake exceeds output, a person will gain weight. When output exceeds input, a person will lose weight. This relationship is called the *energy-balance equation.*

The concept of weight management hinges on this balance. If people want to lose weight, they have to expend more calories than they consume, an essential element of any WEIGHT-LOSS STRATEGY. To gain weight, they have to take in more calories than they use, the basis of any WEIGHT-GAIN STRATEGY.

The key to weight management is to increase or decrease these variables depending on your current practices. To lose weight, you need to decrease your calorie intake, increase your physical activity, or both. A pound (0.5 kg) of fat tissue equals roughly 3,500 calories. For every pound you want to lose, you have to adjust your balance of energy so you burn 3,500 calories more than you consume. To gain weight, you have to reverse the balance. For every pound you want to gain, you have to take in 3,500 calories more than you use. Moderate exercise will help convert the extra calories to muscle instead of fat.

To determine whether you need to lose weight, gain weight, or improve your body composition, you need to do a WEIGHT ASSESSMENT. This will take into account both your weight and your body composition.

Eating Right to Manage Weight   To maintain your weight, you need to eat the same number of calories that you burn. However, all calories are not created equal. The best diet for weight management is one that is

HEALTHY CHOICES
●●●●●●●●●●●●●

high in CARBOHYDRATES, low in FATS, and contains all the NUTRIENTS the body needs. Your diet should include plenty of whole grains, fresh fruits, and vegetables. You should avoid fatty foods that are high in calories and low in nutrients, such as FAST FOODS, JUNK FOODS, fatty meats, and rich desserts. A healthy diet should be a way of life, not just a short-term change.

HEALTHY CHOICES

Using Exercise to Manage Weight   EXERCISE is essential to weight management and good health. Exercise can help people lose weight and (in some activities) gain muscle. In addition to burning extra calories, it strengthens the heart and lungs, and increases general well-being.

According to the American College of Sports Medicine, the best exercise program for weight management includes AEROBIC EXERCISE that is performed at least three times a week for a minimum of 20 minutes each time. People should choose activities they enjoy so they will make exercise a regular part of their lives. An exercise program must be both regular and consistent to be effective. (See also DIETS; ENERGY, FOOD; ENERGY, PHYSICAL; RISK FACTORS.)

▶ WEIGHT TRAINING

Weight training is a form of exercise that uses heavy weights to build muscle mass and improve muscular STRENGTH and ENDURANCE. At one time, only body builders and football players participated in weight training. With the growth of health clubs for men and women and the development of exercise machines, weight training has become popular with other people seeking to improve FITNESS and physical appearance.

HEALTHY CHOICES

Benefits of Weight Training   In addition to building muscle, weight training may build bone mass, which may help prevent osteoporosis, the loss of bone mass that often occurs in older people. By itself, weight training does little to improve cardiovascular fitness. A combination of weight training and AEROBIC EXERCISE, however, can increase strength, muscular and cardiovascular endurance, and overall fitness.

How It Is Done   Weight training involves performing a routine of *isotonic exercises,* exercises that contract each muscle against resistance through a range of motion. Any weight-training program is based on three principles: *overload,* or pushing the muscles to near-maximum effort; *progression,* or adding weight or repetitions as the individual gains strength and endurance; and *balance,* or developing all muscle groups equally.

Weight trainers work out with *free weights,* such as barbells and dumbbells, or with EXERCISE MACHINES, such as Nautilus, Cybex, and Universal machines. Weight training on machines involves exercising a different muscle group at each station of each machine. Some weight trainers circuit-train, which means that they move quickly from one station or lift to the next. By greatly reducing the resting time between exercises, *circuit training* raises a person's heart rate, providing some aerobic effect.

Depending on how it is done, weight training can be adjusted toward developing strength over endurance, or the other way around. At its

Lifting Safely. *When lifting heavy weights, always work with a spotter—a partner who can prevent you from being injured if you lose control of the weights.*

simplest, strength training puts an emphasis on using maximum weight loads, and endurance training emphasizes doing more repetitions of a given exercise using less weight.

Weight Training Safety   At the beginning of a weight-training program, it is wise to work with a trainer or physical education teacher to establish an exercise routine and workout schedule and proper technique. Each session should start with 5 to 10 minutes of warm-up exercise. After lifting, allow for a brief cool-down period as well. To prevent injuries when lifting heavy weights, always work with a partner, or spotter. The spotter's job is to step in and help if you lose control of the weights. Finally, be sure to rest each group of muscles at least a full day between workout sessions. (See also FITNESS TRAINING; STRENGTH EXERCISES.)

▷ **WELLNESS**

Wellness is a state of physical, mental, and emotional well-being. People achieve wellness by making choices that enable them to enjoy life to the fullest.

Every day people make decisions that affect their health. They decide what to eat, how to spend their time, and whom to spend their time with. Most days they also decide how to cope with particular problems or how to plan for future needs. These and many other decisions contribute to an individual's LIFESTYLE. Wellness is achieved by making those lifestyle decisions that are best for overall health.

The concept of wellness is closely related to the idea of preventive medicine. In both cases, the focus is on making choices that reduce the chances of illness and enhance a person's physical, mental, and emotional well-being. (See also PREVENTIVE MEDICINE, **9.**)

SUPPLEMENTARY SOURCES

Brody, Jane. 1981. *Jane Brody's nutrition book*. New York: W. W. Norton Co.

Clark, Nancy. 1990. *Nancy Clark's sports nutrition guidebook*. Champaign, Ill.: Leisure Press.

Coleman, Ellen. 1988. *Eating for endurance*. Emeryville, Calif.: Publishers Group West.

Copen, David, and Mark Rubenstein. 1989. *Heartplan: Complete program for total fitness of heart and mind*. New York: McGraw-Hill.

Eagles, Douglas A. 1987. *Nutritional diseases*. New York: Franklin Watts.

Glover, Bob, and Jack Shepherd. 1989. *The family fitness handbook*. New York: Penguin.

Horovitz, E. 1990. *Cholesterol control made easy: How to lower your cholesterol for a healthier heart*. Los Angeles: Health Trend Publishing.

Kane, June. 1990. *Coping with diet fads*. New York: Rosen Publishing Group.

Kettelkamp, Larry. 1986. *Modern sports science*. New York: William Morrow.

Kolodny, Nancy J. 1987. *When food's a foe: How to confront and conquer eating disorders*. New York: Little, Brown.

Lee, Sally. 1990. *New theories on diet and nutrition*. New York: Franklin Watts.

Maloney, Michael, and Rachel Kranz. 1991. *Straight talk about eating disorders*. New York: Facts On File.

Mayer, Jean. 1990. *Diet and nutrition guide*. New York: Pharos Books.

Quincy, Matthew. 1991. *Diet right! The consumer's guide to diet and weight loss programs*. Berkeley, Calif.: Conari Press.

Roth, Eli M., and Sandra L. Streicher. 1989. *Good cholesterol, bad cholesterol*. Rocklin, Calif.: Prima Publishing & Communications.

Sherman, Roberta T., and Ron A. Thompson. 1990. *Bulimia: A guide for family and friends*. Lexington, Mass.: Lexington Books.

Sleamaker, Rob. 1989. *Serious training for serious athletes*. Champaign, Ill.: Leisure Press.

Tracy, Lisa. 1987. *The gradual vegetarian*. New York: Dell.

ORGANIZATIONS

American Academy of Pediatrics
141 Northwest Point Boulevard
P.O. Box 927
Elk Grove Village, IL 60009
(708) 228-5005

American Anorexia/Bulimia Association
418 East 76th Street
New York, NY 10021
(212) 734-1114

American Diabetes Association
1660 Duke Street
Alexandria, VA 22314
(703) 549-1500

American Dietetic Association
216 West Jackson Boulevard
Chicago, IL 60606
(312) 899-0040

American Heart Association
7320 Greenville Avenue
Dallas, TX 75231
(214) 373-6300

American Running and Fitness Association
4405 East-West Highway
Suite 405
Bethesda, MD 20814
(800) 776-2732

Asthma and Allergy Foundation of America
1717 Massachusetts Avenue
Washington, DC 20036
(202) 265-0265

Center for Chronic Disease Prevention and Health Promotion
Centers for Disease Control
4770 Buford Highway, NE
Atlanta, GA 30341
(404) 488-5080

Food and Drug Administration
Office of Consumer Affairs
5600 Fishers Lane
Rockville, MD 20857
(301) 443-3170

Food and Nutrition Board
Institute of Medicine
2101 Constitution Avenue, NW
Washington, DC 20418
(202) 334-2238

Food and Nutrition Information Center
National Agricultural Library
Room 304
10301 Baltimore Boulevard
Beltsville, MD 20705
(301) 504-5719

International Center for Sports Nutrition
502 South 44th Street
Suite 3012
Omaha, NE 68105
(402) 559-5505

National Handicapped Sports
1145 19th Street, NW
Washington, DC 20036
(301) 652-7505

National Wheelchair Athletic Association
3595 East Fountain Boulevard
Colorado Springs, CO 80910
(719) 574-1150

Office of Disease Prevention and Health Promotion
National Health Information Center
P.O. Box 1133
Washington, DC 20013
(800) 336-4797

Overeaters Anonymous
P.O. Box 92870
Los Angeles, CA 90009
(213) 542-8363

President's Council on Physical Fitness
and Sports
701 Pennsylvania Avenue, NW
Suite 250
Washington, DC 20004
(202) 272-3430

Special Olympics International
1350 New York Avenue, NW
Washington, DC 20005
(202) 628-3630

INDEX

Italicized page numbers refer to illustrations or charts.

Abrasions, 103–4
Additives, food, 52–53
Adrenaline, basal metabolic rate and, 16
Aerobic dance, 4. *See also* Aerobic exercise; Endurance; Fitness training; Flexibility; Heart rate
Aerobic exercise, 4–6, 39–40
   endurance and, 35, 50
   fitness and, 49
   fitness training and, 50
   training for sports and, 100
   for weight management, 132
   See also Cycling; Flexibility; Running; Sports and fitness; Strength; Swimming; Walking
Age, basal metabolic rate and, 16
Agricultural chemicals, 6–7, 86. *See also* Food additives; Food safety
Alcoholics, malnutrition among, 75
Allergies, food, 53–54
Amino acids, 14, 76, 90
Amphetamine, 27
Anabolic steroids, 13
Anabolism, 15
Anaerobic exercise, 5, 7, 40. *See also* Aerobic exercise; Endurance; Fitness; Fitness training; Strength exercise; Weight training
Anaphylactic shock, food allergy and, 53
Anemia, 70, 117
Annatto extract, 53
Anorexia, 8, 33–34, *33*
Antibodies
   in breast milk, 18, 19
   food allergies and, 53
Antimicrobials, 52
Antioxidants, 10, 52, 89, 117, 119
Appetite, 8, 68. *See also* Diets; Eating disorders; Food craving; Hunger; Weight management
Appetite suppressants, 8, 27
Artificial sweeteners, 8–9, 11, 52. *See also* Diet food; Sugar
Ascorbic acid. *See* Vitamin C
Aspartame, 9
Atherosclerosis, cholesterol and, 23
Athletes, diets for, 31
Athletic footwear, 9–10, 96, 106

Back problems, sports and, 102, *103*
Bacterial contamination, 62
Bacterial food poisoning, 57–58
Balance in weight training, 132
Ballistic stretching, 109
Basal metabolic rate, 15–16, 37–38, *37*
Beta carotene, 10, 65, 116. *See also* Nutrients; Vitamins

Beverages, 10–12, 123
Bicycle riding. *See* Cycling
Binge eating, 34
Bioelectrical impedance, 14, 127
Biofeedback, 94
Bioflavonoids, 118
Biotin, *116,* 117, *121*
Blisters, sports and, 103
Blood proteins, 91
Blood sugar level, 67
Body building, 12–13. *See also* Anaerobic exercise; Strength exercise; Weight training
Body composition, 13–14
   body building and changing, 13
   fitness and, 49
   managing, 131
   measuring, 14
   weight assessment and, 124
   See also Diets; Eating disorders; Obesity
Body fat, 13, 14–15, 35–36. *See also* Body composition; Cholesterol; Energy, food; Fats, oils, and sweets group; Risk factors
Body image, 33, 124
Body-mass index (BMI), 14, 87, 126, *126*
Body metabolism, 15–17
   fasting and, 43–44
   measuring, 15–16
   obesity and, 85
   protein and, 91
   See also Digestion; Nutrients
Body temperature
   basal metabolic rate and, 16
   sports and heat problems, 101–2
Body types, *14*
Bomb calorimeter, 20
Bone strength, 49
Botulism, 52, 57–58, 63
Bran, 17
Breads and cereals group, 17–18, 50, *51,* 60, 64, *64. See also* Exchange system; Five food groups system; Food pyramid system; Four food groups system; Starch
Breast-feeding, 18
Breast milk, 18–19
Breathing exercises, 94
Brown rice, 18
Brown sugar, 111
Bruises, 103
Bulimia, 33, 34
Butterfat, 78

Caffeine, 11, 12
Calcium, 19–20, 31, 79, *80,* 114. *See also* Minerals; Vitamins

Calcium deficiency, 19–20
Calcium phosphate, 19
Calcium sorbate, 52
Calorie(s), 20–21
   diet and supply of, 30
   empty, 70, 97
   energy-balance equation, 20–21, 36, 131
   in fats, 45
   junk food and, 70–71
   measuring food energy by, 36
   requirements for energy, 37–38, *37*
   to support basal metabolism, 15–16
   weight-gain strategy and, 128
   weight-loss strategy and, 129
   weight management and, 131
   See also Body metabolism; Diets
Cancer, macrobiotic diet and, 73
Canning, 59
Carbohydrates, 21–22, *36,* 83, *83*
   complex, 21, 22, 106–7
   craving for foods high in, 54
   simple, 21, 22, 106
   See also Breads and cereals group; Energy, food; Fiber; Fruits and vegetables group; Glucose; Nutrients; Starch; Sugar
Cardiovascular endurance, 34, 35, 49
Cardiovascular fitness, 4, 5, 6, 68, 100
Catabolism, 15
Celiac disease, diet for, 32
Cereals, 17
Chafing, 103
Chemical preservation, 52, 59–60, 63
Chemicals, agricultural, 6–7, 86
Children, malnutrition among, 74–75
Chinese restaurant syndrome, 82
Chloride, 79–80
Cholesterol, 5, 23–24, *24,* 45, 47, 77. *See also* Body fat; Fast food; Food labeling; Meats, eggs, and legumes group; Obesity; Risk factors
Chromium, *80,* 81
Circuit training, 132
Cleanliness, food preparation and, 62
Clostridium botulinum, 57
Clostridium perfringens, 57
Coffee, 12
Cold method of food preservation, 59
Coloring agents, 53
Colostrum, 19
Complementary proteins, 76
Complete proteins, 76, 90
Complex carbohydrates, 21, 22, 106–7
Contamination of food, 62–63
Contract-relax stretching, 109–10, *109*
Cooking vegetables, 65–66

Copper, *80*, 81
Cow's milk, sensitivity to, 54
Cramps, 103
Craving, food, 54–55
Cream, 78
Cross-country ski machines, 41
Cross training, 24–25. *See also* Aerobic exercise; Exercise; Fitness; Fitness training; Sports and fitness; Weight training
Cultured milk products, 78
Cyclamate, 9
Cycling, 25–26
    on stationary bicycles, 40–41
    See also Fitness; Fitness training; Heart rate

Dairy products. *See* Milk and milk products group
Dance, aerobic, 4
Dehydration, 26–27, 124
    sweating and, 26, 88, 101
    See also Beverages; Sports and heat problems
Diabetes mellitus, malnutrition and, 74
Diabetic diet, 32
Diarrhea, traveler's, 58
Diet aids, 27–28. *See also* Appetite; Calorie(s); Dietary guidelines; Diets; Exercise; Fad diets; Fiber; Lifestyle; Liposuction; Nutrition; Obesity; Weight-loss strategy; Weight management
Dietary guidelines, 28–29, *28*, 46. *See also* Calorie(s); Cholesterol; Food group systems; Recommended dietary allowance (RDA); Nutrition; Nutrients; Weight management
Dietetics, 85
Diet foods, 27, 29–30. *See also* Appetite; Calorie(s); Diet aids; Dietary guidelines; Diets; Fats; Food labeling; Obesity; Weight-loss strategy; Weight management
Dietitians, 85
Diets, 30–32
    carbohydrates in, 22
    controlling cholesterol with, 24
    elements of healthy, 30
    exchange system for planning, 38–39
    food pyramid system to plan, 60–61
    malnutrition caused by deficiencies in, 73–74
    risk factors in, 30, 95
    to treat and prevent illness, 31–32
    types of, 30–32, 42, 98–99
    water in, 123
    weight assessment and, 127
    for weight management, 131–32
    See also Appetite; Diet foods; Dietary guidelines; Fad diets; Fiber; Food group systems; Nutrition; Phytochemicals; Vegetarian diet
Diet success rate, *129*
Digestion, 32–33, 54. *See also* Appetite; Body metabolism; Energy, food; Hunger
Digestive system, processes of, 32

Disaccharide, 110, 111
Disease, malnutrition caused by, 74
Diuretics, 27
D-limonene, 89
DNA, 117
Drying, food preservation by, 59

Eating disorders, 8, 33–34, 74. *See also* Fasting; Food craving; Malnutrition; Underweight; Weight assessment
Edema, 124
Eggs, *Salmonella* contamination of, 62
Elderly, malnutrition among the, 75
Electric conductivity, 14, 127
Empty calories, 70, 97
Emulsifiers, 53
Endurance, 34–35, 49
    aerobic exercise for, 35, 50
    cardiovascular, 34, 35, 49
    muscular, 34, 35, 49, *99*, 100
    See also Exercise; Fitness; Strength exercise; Weight training
Energy, food, 14–15, 35–36. *See also* Body metabolism; Calorie(s); Energy, physical; Nutrients; Weight management
Energy, physical, 36–38, *37*. *See also* Energy, food; Exercise; Nutrients; Rest; Weight management
Energy-balance equation, 20–21, 36, 131
Enriched breads, 17
Enzymes
    food spoilage and, 59
    muscular endurance and, 35
Ergometers, 41
Escherichia coli, diarrhea from, 58
Essential amino acids, 76, 90
Exchange system, 38–39. *See also* Dietary guidelines; Five food groups system; Food group systems; Food pyramid system; Four food groups system
Exercise, 39–40
    body composition and, 13
    calories and energy expenditure in, 20–21
    cross training, 24–25
    fitness and, 48
    forms of, 39–40
    health and, 39
    lifestyle and, 40
    metabolic rate and, 16, 17
    precautions about, 40
    relaxation after, 93
    risk factors based on, 95
    sweating and fluid replacement during, 26, 88, 101, 102
    to treat obesity, 86
    weight-loss strategy and, 129
    weight management and, 132
    See also Aerobic dance; Aerobic exercise; Anaerobic exercise; Energy, physical; Exercise machines; Fitness training; Risk factors; Sports and fitness; Sports and heat problems; Sports injuries; Sports medicine; Strength exercise; Walking

Exercise machines, 40–42, 132. *See also* Cross training; Endurance; Fitness training; Weight training

Fad diets, 42–43, 130. *See also* Diet aids; Diets; Fasting; Malnutrition; Obesity; Weight management
Fast food, 43. *See also* Fats, oils, and sweets group; Junk food
Fasting, 43–44. *See also* Fad diets; Weight-loss strategy
Fat, body. *See* Body fat
Fat cells, 15, 72
Fatfold measurement, 14, 126
Fatigue, 44–45. *See also* Malnutrition
Fats, 45–46, *46*, 83, *83*
    in fast foods, 43
    low-fat diet, 31
    in meat, eggs, and legumes group, 77
    saturated, 24, *24*, 45, *46*, 47, 77
    unsaturated, 45–46
    vegetarian diet and, 115
    weight-gain strategy and, 128
    See also Body fat; Carbohydrates; Energy, food; Fats, oils, and sweets group; Nutrients; Obesity; Proteins
Fats, oils, and sweets group, 46–47, 51, 60. *See also* Dietary guidelines; Exchange system; Food group systems
Fat-soluble vitamins, 118, 119, 120, *121*, 122
Fatty acids, 14, 36
Fertilizers, 6, 86
Fiber, 21, 47–48, *48*
    low- and high-fiber diets, 31–32
    vegetarian diet and, 115
    See also Carbohydrates; Dietary guidelines
Fish, 75–76
Fitness, 48–49
    body metabolism and, 17
    cardiovascular, 4, 5, 6, 68, 100
    President's Council on Physical Fitness and Sports, 90
    swimming for, 112
    See also Aerobic exercise; Body composition; Endurance; Flexibility; Sports and fitness; Strength; Walking; Weight assessment
Fitness training, 49–50. *See also* Cross training; Energy, physical; Sports and fitness
Five food groups system, 50–51. *See also* Dietary guidelines; Exchange system; Food group systems; Food pyramid system; Four food groups system
Flat breads, 17
Flavoring agents, 52. *See also* Artificial sweeteners; Monosodium glutamate (MSG)
Flexibility, 13, 49, 51–52
    stretching exercise for, 50, 51–52
    See also Fitness training; Sports injuries; Strength exercise
Fluoride, *80*, 81
Folic acid, *116*, 117, *121*

Folk medicine, 89
Food additives, 52–53, 63. *See also* Food allergies; Food labeling; Food preservation methods; Food safety; Organic food
Food allergies, 53–54
Food and Drug Administration (FDA), 8, 27, 29, 47, 52, 53, 57
Food and Nutrition Board of National Academy of Sciences, 56
Food craving, 54–55, *55. See also* Appetite; Weight management
Food energy. *See* Energy, food
Food group systems, 55–56
    exchange system, 38–39
    five food groups system, 50–51
    food pyramid system, 60–61
    four food groups system, 64–65, *64*
    See also Breads and cereals group; Dietary guidelines; Fats, oils, and sweets group; Fruits and vegetables group; Meats, eggs, and legumes group; Milk and milk products group
Food intolerance, 54
Food labeling, 56–57
    for diet foods, 29
    for organic foods, 86
    RDAs and, 56, 93
    for snack foods, 97
    for sodium, 99
    See also Dietary guidelines
Food poisoning, 57–58, 62, 63. *See also* Food safety
Food preservation methods, 52, *53,* 59–60. *See also* Food safety
Food product dating, 57
Food pyramid system, 60–61, *61. See also* Dietary guidelines; Exchange system; Five food groups system; Food group systems; Four food groups system; Nutrients
Food safety, 58, *58,* 61–63. *See also* Food allergies; Food labeling
Food spoilage, 59
Foot problems, sports and, 103, *103*
Fortified cereals, 17
Four food groups system, 64–65, *64. See also* Dietary guidelines; Exchange system; Five food groups system; Food group systems; Food pyramid system
Free radicals, 10, 89, 117, 119
Free weights, 42, 132
Freeze-drying, 59
Freezing method of preserving foods, 59
Fructose, 111
Fruit drinks, 11–12
Fruits and vegetables group, 50–51, 60, 64, *64,* 65–66. *See also* Dietary guidelines; Exchange system; Five food groups system; Food pyramid system; Four food groups system

Garlic, benefits of, 88–89
Glucagon, 67
Glucose, 14, 15, 35, 66–67, 106, 111. *See also* Body metabolism; Digestion; Energy, food; Energy, physical

Glycogen, 35, 66
Goiter, 96
Gout, low-purine diet for, 32
Grains. *See* Breads and cereals group
Group weight-loss programs, 130
Growth regulators, 7

HDL cholesterol, 5, 23
Heart, strength of, 49
Heart disease, excess body fat and, 15
Heart rate, 5, 68
    target range, 6, 68
    See also Aerobic exercise; Fitness; Fitness training; Running; Sports and fitness
Heat cramps, 101
Heat exhaustion, 101
Heatstroke, 101–2
Height and weight chart, 125, *125*
Hemoglobin, iron in, 69
Hepatitis, 58
Heredity and environment, risk factors involving, 94–95
High-density lipoprotein (HDL), 23
    HDL cholesterol, 5, 23
Histamines, 53
Honey, 111
Hormones
    body metabolism and, 15, 16
    growth regulators mimicking, 7
Hunger, 8, 68–69
Hydrogenation, 46
Hydrostatic weighing, 14, 126–27
Hyperglycemia, 67
Hypertension, sodium in diet and, 98
Hypoglycemia, 67
Hypothalamus, sense of hunger and, 69

Incomplete proteins, 76, 90
Ingredients, list of, 56, 71
Injuries. *See* Sports injuries
Insecticides, food contamination by, 58
Insects, food contamination by, 62
Insoluble fibers, 47
Insoluble proteins, 91
Insulin, blood sugar level and, 67
Iodine, 80, *80,* 96
Iron, 69–70, 80, *80*
Iron deficiency, 69–70, 114
Iron-deficiency anemia, 70
Irradiation, 60
Isokinetic exercise, 108
Isometric exercise, 108
Isotonic exercise, 108, 132

Juices, 11–12
Junk food, 70–71. *See also* Fast food; Fats, oils, and sweets group; Food labeling; Recommended dietary allowance (RDA); Snack food

Kilocalorie, 20
Knee injuries, 103, *103*
Kwashiorkor, 73–74

Labeling, food. *See* Food labeling
Lacerations, 103–4
Lactic acid, 7
Lactoovovegetarians, 113
Lactose, 111
Lactose intolerance, 54, 78, 111
Lactovegetarians, 113
Lanugo, 33
Laxatives, 27
LDL cholesterol, 23, 24
Legumes, 76, 107
Lifestyle, 71–72
    as controllable risk factor, 95
    exercise and, 40
    weight management and, 132
    wellness and, 133
    See also Diets; Rest
Lipids, 14–15
Lipoproteins, 23
Liposuction, 72. *See also* Body composition
Liquid diets, 42
Low-density lipoprotein (LDL), 23
    LDL cholesterol, 23, 24
Low-impact aerobics, 6
Low-salt (low-sodium) diet, 31, 98–99
Lungs, aerobic exercise and, 5

Macrobiotic diet, 72, 73, *73. See also* Diets; Fad diets
Macrominerals, 79
Macronutrients, 21, 45, 82, 83, *83,* 90. *See also* Carbohydrates; Fats; Proteins
Magnesium, 79, *80*
Malnutrition, 73–75. *See also* Anemia; Eating disorders; Nutrition; Underweight
Mammary glands, 18
Manganese, *80,* 81
Marasmus, 74
Maximum heart rate, 68
Meats, eggs, and legumes group, 50, 51, 64, *64,* 75–77. *See also* Dietary guidelines; Exchange system; Food group systems
Meat thermometer, using, 62
Meditation, 94
Menstrual cycle, cravings during, 54
Metabolism, 66. *See also* Body metabolism
Microminerals, 79
Micronutrients, 82, *83,* 84. *See also* Minerals; Vitamins
Microorganisms, food spoilage and, 59
Milk, breast, 18–19
Milk and milk products group, 12, 50, 51, 64, *64,* 77–78. *See also* Dietary guidelines; Exchange system; Food group systems
Minerals, 65, 77, 79–81, *80, 83,* 84. *See also* Body metabolism; Calcium; Iron; Nutrients; Potassium; Sodium; Vitamins
Molybdenum, *80,* 81
Monosaccharide, 107, 110, 111
Monosodium glutamate (MSG), 52, 53, 82, 98. *See also* Food additives; Salt
Monounsaturated fats, 46, *46*

MSG. *See* Monosodium glutamate (MSG)
Muscles
    aerobic exercise and, 5
    body building and, 12–13
Muscle strength, 48–49
Muscular endurance, 34, 35, 49, *99*, 100
Myoglobin, 69

National Cancer Institute, 10, 89
National Cholesterol Education Program, 24
National Institutes of Health, *129*
Natural food. *See* Organic food
Nervous system, proteins and regulation of, 91
Niacin, *116*, 117, *121*
Nitrites, 52, 53
Nutrients, 82–84, *83*
    added to foods, 52
    from breads and cereals, 17
    from breast milk, 18, 19
    diet and supply of, 30
    digestion and, 32
    from fruits and vegetables, 65–66
    from meats, eggs, and legumes group, 76–77
    from milk and milk products, 77
    RDA of, *80*, 92–93, *121*, 122
    See also Carbohydrates; Fats; Minerals; Proteins; Vitamins
Nutrition, 84–85. *See also* Body metabolism; Malnutrition; Nutrients; Phytochemicals
Nutritional therapy, 85
Nutritionists, 85
Nutrition labeling, 56–57, *57*

Obesity, 85–86, 128. *See also* Body metabolism; Diet aids; Diet foods; Diets; Overweight; Risk factors; Weight assessment; Weight management
Oils. *See* Fats, oils, and sweets group
Organic food, 86. *See also* Agricultural chemicals; Food safety
Organ meats, 75
Orthopedists, 105
Orthotic devices, 10, 106
Osteomalacia, 119
Osteoporosis, 19
Overload, 108, 132
Overweight, 87, 128–30. *See also* Obesity; Weight assessment; Weight-loss strategy
Oxygen debt, 7, 40

Pancreas, blood sugar level and, 67
Pantothenic acid, *116*, 117, *121*
Parasites, foods contaminated by, 58
Pasta, 18
Pasteurization, 59
Perishable foods, 62
Perspiration, 26, 87–88. *See also* Beverages; Dehydration; Sports and heat problems
Pesticides, 7, 58, 86
Phenylketonuria, *9*

Phenylpropanolamine, 27
Phosphorus, 79, *80*
Physical energy. *See* Energy, physical
Physiological cravings, 54–55
Phytochemicals, 88–89. *See also* Beta carotene; Fiber; Minerals; Vitamin B complex; Vitamin C; Vitamin E
Phytosterols, 89
Pickling, 60
Podiatrists, 106
Polyunsaturated fats, 46, *46*
Potassium, 79, *80*, 89. *See also* Minerals; Sodium
Poultry, 75
Poverty, malnutrition and, 75
Pregnancy, cravings during, 54
Preservatives, 52, 59–60, 63
President's Council on Physical Fitness and Sports, 90. *See also* Exercise; Fitness training; Sports and fitness
Preventive medicine, 133
Processed meats, 75
Progression in weight training, 132
Progressive muscle relaxation, 94
Pronation, 10
Propyl gallate, 52
Protein-calorie malnutrition, 74
Proteins, 83, *83*, 76, 90–92, *91*
Psychological cravings, 55, *55*
Pulse, taking a, 68
Purchasing food, 63
Pyridoxine (B₆), *116*, 117, *121*

Quick breads, 17

Recommended dietary allowance (RDA), 92–93
    on food labels, 56, 92, 93
    of minerals, *80*
    of vitamins, *121*, 122
    See also Dietary guidelines
Recuperation, 94
Refrigeration, 59
Relaxation, 93–94
Reservatrol, 89
Resistance equipment, 42
Rest, 93–94. *See also* Energy, physical; Fatigue; Lifestyle
Resting heart rate, 68
Retinol. *See* Vitamin A
Riboflavin, *116*, 117, *121*
Rice, 17
RICE (Rest, Ice, Compress, Elevate), 102
Rickets, 19, 119
Risk factors, 94–95
Rodents, food contamination by, 62
Roughage. *See* Fiber
Rowing machines, 41
Running, 24, 95–96. *See also* Aerobic exercise; Body composition; Endurance; Fitness; Heart rate; Sports injuries

Saccharin, 8–9
Safety
    cycling, 25–26
    food, 58, 61–63

    running, 96
    weight training, 133
Salmonella food poisoning, 57, 62
Salt, 96–97, 98
    low-sodium (low-salt) diet, 31, 98–99
    as preservative, 52
    See also Minerals; Monosodium glutamate (MSG); Potassium
Satiety, 8
Saturated fats, 24, *24*, 45, *46*, 47, 77
Scurvy, 73, 117
Selenium, *80*, 81
Semivegetarians, 113
Set-point theory of weight, 16
Shellfish, 76
Shinsplints, *103*, 104
Simple carbohydrates, 21, 22, 106
Ski machine, 41
Sleep, 93
Snack food, 97. *See also* Fast food; Junk food; Weight management
Sodium, 79, *80*, 89, 97–99. *See also* Calcium; Potassium; Vitamins; Water
Sodium bicarbonate (baking soda), 98
Sodium chloride. *See* Salt
Sodium propionate, 52
Soft drinks, 11
Soluble fiber, 47
Soluble proteins, 91
Sore muscles, 104
Sports and fitness, 99–101, *99*
    athletic footwear for, 9–10
    calories burned in various activities, 36
    choosing a sport, 99–100
    training for sports, 100–101
    See also Endurance; Fitness training; Flexibility; Sports injuries; Strength
Sports and heat problems, 101–2. *See also* Dehydration; Exercise; Perspiration
Sports injuries, 25, 102–5, *103*
    common types of, 102–4
    treating and preventing, 104–5, 106
    See also Athletic footwear; Sports medicine; Strength exercise; Stretching exercise
Sports medicine, 105–6. *See also* Sports injuries
Sports psychologists, 106
Sprains and strains, sports and, *103*, 104
Sprue, nontropical, 32
Stamina. *See* Endurance
Staphylococcus aureus, food poisoning caused by, 57
Starch, 21, 106–7. *See also* Breads and cereals group; Carbohydrates; Energy, food; Nutrients
Static stretching, 109, *109*
Stationary bicycles, 40–41
Sterilization, 59
Steroids, anabolic, 13
Stimulants, 27
Strength, 48–49, *99*, 100, 107. *See also* Exercise; Fitness; Strength exercise; Weight training

Strength exercise, 49, 100, 107, 108–9, *109. See also* Body building
Stress, relaxation to reduce, 93, 94
Stretching exercise, 40, 100, 109–10
    for flexibility, 50, 51–52
    See also Aerobic dance; Fitness; Running
Sucrose, 111
Sugar, 110–11
    as preservative, 52
    as simple carbohydrate, 21
    in soft drinks, 11
    See also Artificial sweeteners; Carbohydrates; Energy, food; Fats, oils, and sweets group; Fiber; Overweight; Starch
Sulphur, 81
Sulphuraphane, 89
Supination, 10
Surgery, weight loss through, 27–28
Sweat, 87–88, 101
    dehydration and, 26, 88, 102
Sweets. *See* Fats, oils, and sweets group
Swimming, 24, 112–13

Target heart rate, 6, 68
Tartrazine, 53
Tea, 12
Team sports, 100
Temperature, basal metabolic rate and, 16
Tendinitis, sports and, *103*, 104
Thiamine, 116–17, *116*, *121*
Thirst, 26–27, 88, 124
Thyroid gland, overactive, 8
Thyroxine, 27
Trace minerals, 79
Training
    cross, 24–25
    fitness, 49–50
    for sports, 100–101
    strength, 107
    weight, 7, 12, 132–33
Traveler's diarrhea, 58

Treadmills, 41–42
Tuber family, 107

Underweight, 113, 128. *See also* Weight assessment; Weight-gain strategy
Unsaturated fats, 45–46
U.S. Department of Agriculture (USDA), 10, 29, 60
    Research Center on Aging, 89
U.S. Department of Health and Human Services, 29

Vegans, 30, 113
Vegetables. *See* Fruits and vegetables group
Vegetarian diet, 30–31, 72, 73, 113–15. *See also* Diets; Vitamin B complex
Vitamin A, 10, 65, 115–16, *121*
Vitamin A deficiency, 115
Vitamin B$_6$, *116*, 117, *121*
Vitamin B$_{12}$, 114, *116*, 117, *121*
Vitamin B complex, 116–17, *116*
Vitamin C, 52, 65, 117–18, *121*. *See also* Vitamin E
Vitamin D, 114, 118–19, *121*
Vitamin E, 52, 119–20, *121*. *See also* Vitamin C
Vitamin K, 120–21, *121*
Vitamins, *83*, 84, 121–22, *121*
    fat-soluble, 118, 119, 120, *121*, 122
    in fruits and vegetables, 65
    in milk, 77
    RDAs for, *121*, 122
    water-soluble, 118, *121*, 122

Waist-to-hip ratio, 127
Walking, 122–23. *See also* Athletic footwear; Endurance
Water, 11, 123–24
    balance of, 124
    fluid replacement during sports, 102
    foods with high water content, 123
    See also Beverages; Body metabolism; Dehydration; Minerals
Water-soluble vitamins, 118, *121*, 122

Weight assessment, 124–27, *125*
    methods of, 125–27
    See also Body composition; Diets; Eating disorders; Fitness; Obesity; Overweight; Underweight; Weight-gain strategy; Weight-loss strategy
Weight-gain strategy, 30, 113, 128. *See also* Body metabolism; Fats, oils, and sweets group; Underweight; Weight assessment; Weight management
Weight lifting, 108
Weight-loss strategy, 128–30
    diet foods for, 29–30
    diets for, 30
    diet success rates, *129*
    elements of successful, 129–30
    fad diets and, 42–43, 130
    for overweight, 87, 128–30
    strategies to avoid, 130
    to treat obesity, 86, 128
    See also Diet aids; Weight assessment; Weight management
Weight machines, 42
Weight management, 130, 130–32
    body metabolism and, 16, 17
    eating right for, 131–32
    energy-balance equation and, 21, 36, 131
    excess body fat and, 13
    exercise for, 132
    See also Diets; Energy, food; Energy, physical; Lifestyle; Risk factors
Weight training, 7, 12, 132–33. *See also* Endurance; Fitness; Strength
Wellness, 133
White rice, 17
Whole-grain breads, 17

Yeast breads, 17
Yin and yang, 73, *73*
Yo-yo syndrome, 42, 130

Zen macrobiotic diet, 73
Zinc, *80*, 81